For Haig and Andrea

Here's looking forward

to a better year

A SKEIN OF THOUGHT

A SKEIN OF THOUGHT

THE IRELAND AT FORDHAM HUMANITARIAN LECTURE SERIES

Edited by

Brendan Cahill
Johanna Lawton

In collaboration with the
Permanent Mission of Ireland to the United Nations
with funding from the Government of Ireland.

Refuge Press, New York, 2020

ISBN#13: 978-0-8232-9367-4 (Hard Cover)
ISBN#13: 978-0-8232-9368-1 (Paperback)
ISBN#13: 978-0-8232-9366-7 (ePub)

All royalties from this book go to the training of humanitarian workers.

Edited by: Brendan Cahill and Johanna Lawton
Book and Cover Design: Mauro Sarri

Printed in the United States of America.

Table of Contents

Preface

Geraldine Byrne Nason

Permanent Representative of Ireland to the UN

Welcome to the compendium of lectures of the *'Ireland at Fordham Humanitarian Lecture Series.'* The Permanent Mission of Ireland has been proud to collaborate with Fordham University's Institute of International Humanitarian Affairs, in a partnership that speaks to Ireland's profile as a leader in international development and humanitarian action, as well as Fordham's commitment to distinguished research and education.

Over the last 18 months, our collaboration has built upon our shared commitment to exploring the challenges facing policy makers and humanitarian actors working to get aid to the most vulnerable people on our planet, often in the most hard to reach places. COVID-19 has made their job even more difficult. Throughout this lecture series, we have had the honour to hear from a range of eminent speakers, who addressed both established and emerging issues in the humanitarian field.

On this journey, we explored the challenges facing policy makers and humanitarians as they deliver life-saving support and protection to people in need. Addresses by H.E. Mary Robinson, Chair of The Elders and the first woman elected President of Ireland; President Michael D. Higgins; Dr. Jemilah Mahmood, at the time Under-Secretary General at the International Federation of Red Cross and Red Crescent Societies; Chief of the Defence Forces, Vice Admiral Mark Mellett; United Nations Resident Coordinator, Jamie McGoldrick; Dr. Caitriona Dowd; WFP's Matthew Hollingworth; and Tánaiste and Minister for Foreign Affairs and Trade, Simon Coveney, T.D., raised issues including the intersection between humanitarian action and climate justice, activism and the public intellectual, trust and localisation, peacekeeping, humanitarian access, and conflict and hunger.

Since the inaugural lecture by President Mary Robinson at the United Nations in May 2019, we have witnessed the nature of humanitarian need rapidly changing. Conflicts have become more protracted and societies are faced with new and emerging threats such as the devastating impact of COVID-19. As each of our eight lectures demonstrate, we must adapt and improve the delivery of humanitarian assistance to help those in need without delay as humanitarian crises become more and more complex. It is our collective responsibility to ensure the full respect for international humanitarian law in all contexts. Moreover, as is argued with clear conviction in all lectures, it is crucial that humanitarian workers are given the access and support necessary to provide vital assistance to those who need it most.

This series brings an Irish perspective to exploring some of these challenges and how they affect policy makers and humanitarians as they seek to ensure aid reaches those in need, humanitarian principles are upheld, and civilians are protected. Listening to the expert voices of practitioners with first hand experience, the lecture series has helped to inform Ireland's understanding of how these humanitarian issues, arising with ever greater frequency and urgency, interact with the work of the United Nations Security Council, to which we hope to be elected for the term 2021–2022.

Ireland has long been a leader in humanitarian response, from our missionaries to our current steadfast support for the global humanitarian system with the UN at its centre.

I recall the words of President Mary Robinson in her lecture, *"If we all fail to act now; if we fail to act decisively; if we fail to act together; future generations will never forgive us for the world that we bequeath them."* Ireland is committed to a values-based foreign policy, with principled humanitarian action at its very core. Our response to crisis is underpinned by a strong commitment to international humanitarian law and the provision of predictable, flexible, and timely funding, based on the humanitarian principles of independence, neutrality, impartiality, and humanity. These principles ensure that humanitarian assistance is targeted, based on need, and provided without discrimination.

The humanitarian system is an essential pillar of the effective multilateralism to which Ireland is committed. As humanitarian needs increase we need to redouble our support to the current system while looking at how we can prevent needs from arising in the first place, through investments in prevention and development. Reducing humanitarian need is a cornerstone of Ireland's development policy, which was launched earlier this year.

I like to think that Ireland's lived memory of vulnerability as a country that has endured conflict, migration, famine and colonialisation, has helped shape our commitment to a profoundly ethical response to these global challenges. In Ireland we believe in shared responsibility to address those challenges together. Sometimes that means shining a light in dark places, to bring relief to those who needed it most. It is my sincere hope that this Ireland at Fordham Humanitarian Lecture Series does just that, by shining a light on the realities and challenges of the humanitarian space today, so that we may better respond to it tomorrow.

Introduction

Brendan Cahill
Executive Director, IIHA

The Institute of International Humanitarian Affairs was founded at Fordham University to act as a bridge between the academic and humanitarian sectors, which it achieves through training, research, publications, exhibitions, conferences, and global partnerships. In *The Idea of a University*, John Henry Newman wrote:

"It is education which gives a man a clear, conscious view of their own opinions and judgements, a truth in developing them, an eloquence in expressing them, and a force in urging them. It teaches him to see things as they are, to go right to the point, to disentangle a skein of thought to detect what is sophistical and to discard what is irrelevant."

Education and discourse break down the walls that narrow our views, and, by sharing our thoughts and critiquing them, we emerge to a better level of understanding and action. It is with this philosophy that the Institute partnered with the Permanent Mission of Ireland to the United Nations to organize these lectures and to create this book.

In 1841, John Hughes, an Irish migrant who had risen to the highest office in the Catholic Church in New York, founded Fordham University. Hughes was an advocate and an innovator throughout his life. He created the New York parochial school system when he saw children were not being properly educated in the anti-immigrant public schools, he founded the Emigrant Savings Bank when he realized migrants were being denied access to fair banking, and, in Fordham University, he saw that it is education, especially higher education, that allows for social mobility, justice and prosperity for the most vulnerable. Hughes was also a diplomat, traveling to Europe to prevent European powers from interfering in the US Civil War. He lived in a time—as we do now—where the migrant was demonized and victimized and denied their human rights. It was his belief that those who had power also had an obligation to provide for those who had none. He identified protection, education and human rights not as luxuries but as necessities, and, perhaps most importantly, having identified those inequalities, he fought to right them. That ethos informs the work of everything the Institute has done.

Ireland, in its most recent policy paper, *A Better World*, has made a strong and reasoned plan for foreign investment and support. In his introduction to that document, Simon Coveney, T.D., Ireland's Tánaiste and Minister for Foreign Affairs and Trade, stated clearly: *"During our public consultations, we heard that Irish people see development cooperation as an investment in a better future, as an important projection of our values and as a statement of solidarity with others who are less fortunate. It is also important to our safety and security, a protection against volatility in a time of change.*

We believe that the focus in this new policy will help create that better world which we want for ourselves and our children, a world where Ireland shows effective leadership and good global citizenship as we move into the second century of our independence."

Complementing the values of Newman and Hughes, the paper looks at foreign investment as an opportunity for all, to be a voice for those who need one, a trading partner for those who ask for one, a friend for those who seek one. To complement that clear vision, we chose eminent speakers from the United Nations, academia, diplomacy, security, and the Red Cross Movement who represented the very best in their own fields. We worked closely with the Permanent Mission of Ireland to the United Nations to highlight those sectors that represented Irish priorities—climate issues, protection, gender equality, food security, etc. This book is the result.

The concerns raised by the oncoming effects of climate change require nothing less than the complete unity of all nations not just in word but through concerted action. Communities across the world already face drought, food-insecurity, and increasing environmental fragility based upon the human-caused fluctuation in the natural climate. The time to act is now. The Permanent Mission of Ireland and the Institute of International Humanitarian Affairs share a deep bond and a profound commitment to these same values upheld and promoted within the climate justice framework. The example set forward by the Irish determination for the promotion and protection of human rights for all provides this storied institution with a wealth of potential to further stand with our most vulnerable communities. The Founding Charter of the United Nations begins, famously, with *We the Peoples of the United Nations determined to save succeeding generations from the scourge of war…*

We must never forget—even in the face of xenophobia and greed—that we are made stronger by dialogue and action, by what Bertrand Russell called his three passions—the longing for love, the search for knowledge, and the unbearable pity for the suffering of mankind. We celebrate our organizations' deep bonds and shared commitments to human rights and climate justice, while also taking the opportunity to pause and reflect on the difficult path towards a brighter, more equitable future.

Increasingly, humanitarian efforts are recognized empirically, and there has been a necessary move toward greater professionalization in humanitarian assistance. In professionalization, however, we can sometimes lose the overall purpose for the delivery, and sideline the passion of the volunteer for the sake of processes. We need the passion of the volunteer just as importantly as professionalization and accountability. Ireland has sent educators throughout the world for hundreds of years; it is a nation that has been a proud supporter of U.N. Peacekeeping efforts for many decades. It has embraced the multilateral approach to global security and harmony. In 1861, in his first inaugural address, President Lincoln spoke to a country in crisis, appealing to the "better angels of our nature." Words matter, the academy matters, critical thinking matters, inspiration matters. The contributors to these lectures, and to this book, approached these themes in different but complementary ways. President Michael D. Higgins eloquently examined the role of the public intellectual in times of crisis. Admiral Mark Mellett wrote incisively about seeing *"the role of Ireland's Defense Forces contributing to an effort to move institutions along the continuum from insecurity to security, from an absence of peace to peace."* In her chapter on localization, Dr. Jemilah Mahmood examined the movement toward consultation with, and not simply provision to, populations in need. Mr. Jamie McGoldrick decried the increasing politicization of humanitarian assistance and the erosion of humanitarian neutrality.

We are pleased to collaborate with the Permanent Mission of Ireland in working towards a world which ensures the protection of human rights along with a renewed respect for the environment. These shared values both strengthen the bond our organizations share today and serve to guide us for the future. The vision of change laid out by the U.N.'s Sustainable Development goals represent the type of transformative change that The Permanent Mission of Ireland and the Institute of International Humanitarian Affairs support. The path towards these goals will of course face obstacles, as witnessed by pandemics, wars, natural disasters, and sectarian violence that confront us regularly. The way forward is not always clear but the humanitarian values of the Irish state, and those who represent them, serve to indicate how passionately Ireland would represent a multilateral world on the Security Council.

How Climate, Gender and Insecurity Are Driving Food Insecurity and Humanitarian Need

H.E. Mary Robinson,
Chair of the Elders

It is always a pleasure and privilege to return to the United Nations, and it is a particular pleasure to deliver the first "Ireland at Fordham Humanitarian Lecture," which will focus on the challenges facing humanitarian action in the twenty-first century.

Fordham University has a long and venerable connection to Ireland. Indeed, I was delighted, as President of Ireland, to speak at Fordham's Rose Hill campus in 1995 to mark that Institution's 150th Annual Commencement. This new collaboration between Ireland and Fordham will build on their shared commitment to exploring the challenges facing policy-makers and humanitarians in the twenty-first century.

Over the last century, we have made progress in addressing humanitarian and development challenges. However, there are significant risks to our continued progress. Our commitment to strong, multilateral responses to major crises is challenged when we need it most. At the same time, conflicts are increasing in number, becoming more protracted and fragmented, and pushing unprecedented numbers of people into humanitarian need.

I believe climate change—which poses an existential threat to all humanity—is playing an increasingly central and destructive role right across the range of issues that the United Nations strives to address.

As Chair of The Elders, I am dismayed that we could reverse the development gains of the last 100 years, not because we cannot act, but because we will not act. The need to act and act fast is the message of marchers and school children that we have seen in recent months.

We hear these voices not only in the West. While the links between climate, poverty, fragility, and insecurity are only beginning to be fully understood, there is little doubt that the links exist—mostly for those who are living this reality every day. As Hindou Ibrahim, an activist from Chad (and a good friend), told the Security Council last year:

"My people are living climate change. Climate change has an impact on their daily lives and gives them insecurity. When they sleep at night, they dream that they will wake up the next day and be able to get food or water for their children. They also dream that if someone gets to the resources before they do, they will have to fight for them."

Climate change is not just an issue of atmospheric science or plant conservation; it is fundamentally about human rights and the protection of people. When we think about the Universal Declaration of Human Rights and the core principles it promotes, it is abundantly clear that the impacts of climate change are rapidly undermining the full enjoyment and full range of human rights. It is quite often the most vulnerable who are facing loss of their right to life, to food, to safe water, to shelter, and to health.

Last year's Intergovernmental Panel on Climate Change (IPCC) report clearly outlines that our basic human rights stand to be eroded due to the climate crisis: risks to health, livelihoods, food security, water supply, human security, and economic growth are all projected to increase with global warming at 1.5°C and to increase further to a dangerous level with 2°C.

In 2016, as the Secretary-General's Special Envoy for El Niño and Climate, I saw for myself, with Macharia Kamau, who was also a Special Envoy for El Niño and Climate, how existing phenomena such as El Niño and La Niña are compounded by climate change. And, I saw the real humanitarian consequences for poor people—particularly for women.

The evidence is now building; the number of people going to bed and waking up hungry is on the rise. The 2019 Global Report on Food Crises tells us that climate and natural disasters pushed 29 million people into situations of acute food insecurity in 2018, mostly in Africa. Unpredictable seasons in rural areas are dramatically affecting rural people's—especially women's—livelihoods, undermining the ability of farmers to grow and provide food, and the ability of communities to access health and education services. Likewise, the increased frequency and intensity of extreme weather events as a result of climate change is leading to an increase in displacement of people and communities—23.5 million people in 2016 according to the World Meteorological Organization.

I was very moved recently when my fellow Elder, Graça Machel, described the devastation she saw after a recent visit to Beira in her beloved country Mozambique. Mozambique has now been hit by another cyclone, Kenneth. These people do not have a plan B, do not have insurance, do not have reserves that they can look to. They are just devastated...devastated and in poverty, not really knowing where to turn. While estimates of the number of people likely to be displaced as a result of climate change vary, the stark reality is that they will be multiples of those we see today.

The challenge of climate change is not only about droughts and desertification displacing people in Africa. Sea level rise threatens whole communities living in small island developing states. Island countries such as the Maldives and Kiribati are facing the loss of their sovereign islands with rising sea levels. As a result, they are championing the issue of climate change as a human rights challenge, connected to the displacement of people and the potential loss of life, as well as the right to low-carbon development. We must remember that the people and countries bearing the brunt of food insecurity, social instability and forced displacement have not contributed to the main cause of climate change. That is the injustice of climate change. This fact embodies the injustice and the necessity to recapture global justice through more ambitious climate action.

As the President of the IFRC said recently, climate change is already making emergency response efforts around the world more difficult, more unpredictable and more complex. However, we cannot only consider the direct effects of climate change. By undermining livelihoods, eroding food and water security, driving displacement, increasing competition for scarce resources, and increasing economic and gender inequalities, climate change acts as a threat multiplier, pushing already vulnerable and fragile societies over the edge.

With few options available to individuals, particularly young men, economic hardship and marginalization can open the door for the predatory activities of violent extremists in search of recruits.

While no armed conflict has one single driver, there is an increasingly strong body of evidence that suggests that climate change, interacting with other factors, such as political, economic, and social conditions, is a major contributing factor. Armed conflict is now the main reason that nearly 140 million people will need humanitarian assistance and protection this year—most in a small number of countries like Syria, Yemen, and South Sudan.

The role that climate change plays in crises is context-specific. Climate and insecurity interact in already vulnerable contexts and create a vicious cycle leading to increased humanitarian need. As a paper from the Overseas Development Institute and the Red Cross Movement pointed out, "the most severe impacts of climate change are not necessarily in areas exposed to the greatest changes in climate, but in places where people's capacities to cope with these changes are lacking."

Individuals and communities affected by conflict and fragility lack access to social protection or necessary institutional supports. As a result, their resilience is undermined and their ability to adapt reduced. Deputy Secretary-General, Amina Mohammed, told the Security Council last year: "*Fragile countries are in danger of becoming stuck in a cycle of conflict and climate disaster.*" The most frequently cited example of this phenomenon is the situation in the Lake Chad basin region, where an environmental catastrophe—the shrinking of Lake Chad by 90%—has had profound economic and social implications. The shrinking of the lake was accompanied by a shrinking of economic opportunities, an increase in vulnerability, and the rise of instability and violent extremism—most notably, the Boko Haram insurgency. Local leaders, such as Hindou Ibrahim, are in no doubt about the link between these two events.

Disasters are not the only climate change-related developments that affect security. I believe that we must also broaden our perspectives when we consider what we mean by insecurity and the potential for a humanitarian crisis. So-called 'conflict' can manifest at all levels; intra-national conflict, or conflict between major ethnic groups, is worthy of consideration, especially as it leads to displacement, which further exacerbates climate vulnerability and plays havoc with ecosystems. Moreover, lower-level conflict can often have a negative impact, especially placing different kinds of strain on humanitarian systems, including in zones or regions of the world not traditionally associated with conflict.

This reality was acknowledged by the leaders of the Pacific Islands Forum, where they declared, "*Climate change remains the single greatest threat to the livelihoods, security and well-being of the peoples of the Pacific.*" The Pacific Small Island Developing States have pushed hard for the appointment of a Special Envoy on Climate and Security. Their aim is to put in place mechanisms that will allow them to forecast what future security threats might play out as a result of climate impacts in their traditionally peaceful region. This is an initiative I fully support, as it aims to prepare for the future realities we know we will face. The response to date, in terms of how we, as an international community, prepare for the growing humanitarian needs that stem from climate change, has been, I'm afraid, sorely lacking.

The Security Council had its first discussion on climate and security in seven years under the Swedish Presidency of the Security Council last July. This was followed last January with an open debate under the Dominican Republic's Council Presidency. I am acutely aware of the arguments against the Security Council dealing with this issue—encroachment on the mandates of other UN entities, the risk of securitisation of climate change, as well as a denial of climate change itself by some. However, we, The Elders, believe it is time that the Security Council caught up with the reality on the ground—the reality for the communities that Hindou Ibrahim gave voice to when she spoke to the Council.

Understanding climate risk should be an essential element of the Security Council's prevention agenda. By deepening its understanding of how climate change is interacting with other drivers in the individual country contexts on its agenda—or with the potential to reach its agenda—the Council can meet its responsibility under the UN Charter. Doing so does not mean that the Council is encroaching on the mandates of other UN entities, only that it considers all factors at play in a given context.

It is encouraging that the Council has begun to move in this direction, with its recognition of the need for adequate risk assessment and management strategies relating to the adverse security effects of climate and ecological factors in a number of geographical contexts, including the Lake Chad Basin, the Sahel, and the Horn of Africa. However, in order for members of the Council to carry out their work, there is a need for a better understanding of climate related security risks across all of the Council's files. This requires better reporting from the field that includes climate risk assessments as standard. Reporting needs to be integrated with an analysis of how the different drivers of conflict are interacting with one another. The inter-agency initiative established by the Secretary-General is a welcome move in this regard.

Outside of the Security Council, the humanitarian community has recognised the challenges it faces in responding to the growing humanitarian needs as a result of climate change and conflict. The World Humanitarian Summit Chair's summary recognised that humanitarian assistance alone will never adequately address nor sustainably reduce the needs of the world's most vulnerable people; rather, a new coherent approach is required, based on addressing root causes, increasing political diplomacy for prevention and conflict resolution, and bringing humanitarian, development and peacebuilding efforts together.

In my view, there are three elements that are needed to form the basis of this new approach. Firstly, and this won't surprise you, climate justice. This is a concept that I have championed for some time. It links human rights and development to achieve a human-centred—a people centred—approach, safeguarding the rights of the most vulnerable people and sharing the burdens and benefits of climate change and its impacts equitably and fairly. Climate justice is informed by science, responds to science and acknowledges the need for equitable stewardship of the world's resources.

Climate justice is a transformative concept. It insists on a shift from a discourse on greenhouse gases and melting ice caps into a civil rights movement with people and communities most vulnerable to climate impacts at its heart. Humanitarian action must put this concept at the centre of its efforts, particularly when engaging climate related impacts.

Part of this climate justice approach is a recognition of how men and women are affected by climate change in different ways. For example, in many communities women are the primary food producers and providers of water and cooking fuel for their families, so any changes in climate or disasters that affect these roles, not only impact women's ability to provide, but also on the community as a whole. It is for this reason that women must be at the forefront of the response. Women are best placed to identify the needs and vulnerabilities of their communities and should therefore be consulted and involved in decision-making in climate adaptation, humanitarian preparedness, and response.

Climate justice does not just cut across countries and societies. It cuts across generations—how we safeguard future generations. What kind of world do we want to leave to our children and to our grandchildren? Can we proudly stand here today and say that their lives will be more prosperous, more equal and fairer than our own? In fact, tomorrow's leaders may well be frustrated and angry by our inaction today. We need to anticipate and integrate the needs and concerns of future generations to better inform the decisions that we make today.

Secondly, we can no longer afford to regard the 2030 Agenda and the Paris Climate Agreement as voluntary, and a matter for each member state to decide on its own. It is clear from the IPCC report that the full implementation of both the 2030 Agenda and the Paris Climate

Agreement has become imperative in order to save future generations from an increasing level of humanitarian disaster and need. Delivering on the goals we have set ourselves in the 2030 Agenda for Sustainable Development and the Paris Climate Agreement, as well as the Sustaining Peace Agenda, will not eliminate the challenges ahead, but it will significantly improve our ability to address them. At the same time, without reaching the furthest behind, we will never realise the 2030 Agenda.

The more just, equal, sustainable, and prosperous societies envisaged in the 2030 Agenda would be better able to respond to the challenges of climate change. However, delivering on the promise of the SDGs will mean accepting profound changes to the way we live our lives. Are we ready for such a transformation? Making it happen will require a change of mind-set at the global political level.

Limiting the increase in global average temperature to 1.5°C would substantially reduce the risks and effects of climate change, particularly on those communities least able to respond. However, we must ensure that the most vulnerable communities, who face the worst impacts, have access to international support and financing for adaptation to impacts that will happen irrespective of limiting global temperature increases. Likewise, those working in fossil fuel industries cannot be left out. We need more funding for just transition, for adaptation solutions and for technology. The financing is there—I have absolutely no doubt of that. But, we need to work harder and more collectively to make it work for those on the frontlines of climate change.

Rebalancing our approach to peace and security in line with the Sustaining Peace Agenda means investing in early warning and prevention as well as tackling the root causes of conflict, including human rights violations. The Security Council needs to act before the first shots are fired. A 'whole of organisation' approach is needed from the UN, and it must be aligned with inclusive, nationally led processes as well as the efforts of regional organisations. In post-conflict contexts, the Peacebuilding Commission has an important role to play in bringing all of these pieces together.

How do we get this political will? How do we get this sense of global solidarity needed to make this a reality? I believe it is through the emerging movement for climate justice, putting pressure on governments and on business, particularly the fossil fuel industry. It is heartening to see women leaders stepping forward—and they really are stepping forward. Believe me, it's amazing. I'm encouraged by this—school children striking and young people making their voices heard. Some, such as Extinction Rebellion, have taken to peaceful protest, and there's increasing business and investment leadership calling, indeed pressing, for more ambition from governments. Businesses pressing governments—because business does longer-term thinking than government sometimes does. Governments are focused on the next election—six months, a year, two years. The importance of this growing climate justice movement is that it will call for a just transition to a world powered by clean energy, and climate actions that fully respect human rights.

The third point is recognising that we know that climate change will drive humanitarian need. We should, therefore, invest in measures that reduce vulnerabilities and increase preparedness and resilience to shocks, including climate shocks. The Sendai Framework for Disaster Risk Reduction provides a practical and tangible bridge between the development and humanitarian communities to prevent new, and reduce existing, disaster risks. The framework underlines the need for enhanced work to reduce exposure and vulnerability, thus preventing the creation of new disaster risks, and accountability at all levels for disaster risk creation. And most importantly, I believe, it identifies that there has to be a broader and a more people-centred preventive approach to disaster risk. Disaster risk reduction practices need to be multi-hazard and multi-sectoral, inclusive and accessible in order to be efficient and effective.

At the same time, the humanitarian community must continue to explore new tools and innovations that allow it to act early, such as anticipatory financing, cash transfer programming, and disaster risk insurance. We know that early interventions can greatly lessen the impact of climate related shocks—we need to become better at identifying opportunities to intervene before a looming risk transforms into a full blown humanitarian catastrophe. These initiatives should be seen as part of a much broader risk management approach that includes humanitarian, development, security, and climate actors.

The three pillars I have outlined point to the need for an integrated approach, which puts the individual right at the centre of all our actions—not as a subject but as an active participant in their own destiny. This is very much the approach set out in Ireland's new international development policy *A Better World*, in which reducing humanitarian needs sits alongside gender equality, strengthening governance, and climate action as Ireland's policy priorities. These are issues and above that actually, an approach that I expect Ireland to highlight in its campaign for the Security Council in 2021—2022. It's also why I am very supportive of that campaign.

If we all fail to act now; if we fail to act decisively; if we fail to act together, future generations will never forgive us for the world that we bequeath them.

I think a lot about that world. I have six grandchildren; the eldest is fifteen. They will be in their twenties, and their thirties and forties in 2050. They will share the world with nine billion people, and I think a lot about that world and what they will think of us if we do not use the window that we have.

I want to recall the haunting words of Hindou Ibrahim to the Security Council last July:

"For me, as one who comes from these communities, I see babies and young people growing up in this area and think about them in the next decade or the next twenty years. What will their futures be like? Are they also going to jump in the sea? Are they going to join terrorist groups? Or are they going to kill each other because, in order to survive, they have to eat?"

I want to end with the words of the first Chair of The Elders, Archbishop Desmond Tutu, who, when asked if he was an optimist, answered, "*No, but I'm a prisoner of hope.*" Because it is hope we need to give us the energy to go forward resolutely and to accept the challenge of this window of time that we have to transform to a world that will be safe for our children and grandchildren.

—United Nations, April 2019

Humanitarianism and the Public Intellectual in Times of Crisis

Michael D. Higgins
President of Ireland

A chairde,

To make a beginning to this lecture, what I've entitled *"Humanitarianism and the Public Intellectual in Times of Crisis,"* I very much always enjoy returning to an academic environment. And this is perhaps understandable, having been a university teacher for so much of my life. It was a world I found profoundly rewarding and enriching. But there is no place quite like a university for reflection, the hallowed seat of learning, yes, but more importantly, a gathering place of the young and curious who believe that the world need not be as cruel as it is, but indeed, can be changed.

Universities can transform people's lives through education and, of course, through the wider impact of their research. Universities can help students to develop their skills and knowledge, and now, perhaps this is the most important of all, I think now given our interacting crises—ecological, economic, social, and may I suggest ethical—we turn to universities in near desperation to provide a basis to help us for a broader understanding of the interconnectedness of our social-ecological system.

University research, it is claimed, correctly, is potentially of benefit to everyone, with the capacity of intellectual space for enriching society, stimulating culture, and, of course, creating enterprise. However, now it must face its greatest challenge. A moment of truth has arrived for all institutions, including third-level institutions—that of facilitating an exit from a paradigm that has failed humanity and of outlining how we can make our way to a new paradigm that will lead to integrated, sustained eco-social policies of sufficiency and equity. It will no longer be sufficient to train people to run after the bus of disaster, but rather to seek to understand why it is all happening. For what we teach, after all, is the foundation of policy, and subverting the taken for granted, the authoritarian and the socially dangerous must be the core values of a university.

Indeed, I agree with Father McShane and John Hughes, Archbishop of New York, who established this very university St. John's College in 1841, and understood instinctively that education is key to active and enriching citizenship for immigrants and to human flourishing. The story of John Hughes's family is a quintessential Irish-American story: a family who departed Ireland's shores two centuries ago, families, some of whom were forced to leave as a result of hunger or persecution, while others earlier in the 19th century had sought to escape poverty and to build better lives for themselves and their families. Throughout its history, Fordham itself, as an educational institution, has had a commitment to the betterment of society and social justice, both at home and abroad.

In relation to those two waves of migration, it is very important as well to know that the first migration—from which, if you like, John Hughes came—were from South Ulster, North Munster, the many cases, and they paid their fare to come. After the revolution of 1798 and the active union of 1800, there was a rumour that the country was finished. Many people who had the means of anything just simply moved. Any they came early, established themselves early, and so, they would be completely different to the tsunami of the desperate who would come in the 1850s.

In America, and elsewhere across the globe, the Irish found refuge and opportunity. They did not escape either the marginalisation or the exploited fear of the "other" that is the experience now of too many migrants today. They overcame this and went on to contribute to the economic, social, political and cultural development of their adoptive homes, as today's migrants are doing all over the world. Here in the United States, we saw a new Irish-American culture emerge as a result of the mingling of these different strands, as it were, of two rich cultures interacting, creating something that is not reducible to either, but which in its transcendence

combines the best of both heritages.
Today, 17% of Irish citizens are currently living abroad, joining a continuous trend within the 70 million people of Irish descent worldwide. The Irish were not easily to forget, and it is something we must never forget. We too in fact were editorialised in the 1840s, suggesting, for example, that the Irish Famine was an act of God, that the Irish in fact were being punished, as well as that they were backward, a hopeless case. And indeed a brilliant philosopher somewhere a hundred years earlier had said that they had never even been occupied by the Romans, so how could they have the civilities that other people had.
But I think, therefore, they did not convert to these editorials of the 1840s. A mere 12 years later in 1860 you will find, I think in The Times of London, a different editorial appears, and it says:
"If this goes on as it is likely to go on… the United States will become very Irish… So an Ireland there will still be, but on a colossal scale, and in a new world. We shall only have pushed the Celt Westwards. Then, no longer cooped between the Liffey and the Shannon, he will spread from New York to San Francisco, and keep up the ancient feud at an unforeseen advantage…We must gird our loins to encounter the nemesis of seven centuries' misgovernment. To the end of time a hundred million spread over the largest habitable area in the world, and, confronting us everywhere by sea and land, will remember that their forefathers paid tithe to the Protestant clergy, rent to the absentee landlords, and a forced obedience to the laws which these had made."
And thus it was to be in a way, but there is of course a great challenge in that, one with which I have been engaged as President for the first period of my Presidency. That is, how do you make an ethical commemoration? How do you use memory ethically? Which is for a whole other day and anyway, it is all on my website, so there it is.
I think that this question of actually putting the narrative of the other into one's consciousness, in such a way that one is able to read and how one knows, as I said in one of my poems, who knows how

to come to a point where forgiveness might be possible. Our nation's history contains many tragic reminders of the desperate plight of those forced to flee their country—the most acute of which was the Great Famine of the 1840s. One million people died from starvation, further 2.5 million emigrated, the majority to North America, resulting in the halving of the population of the Island of Ireland between 1841 and the early 1900s.

It is important to remember that in the census of 1901, of all the people born within the Island of Ireland, a majority of people were living outside of Ireland. And I think that gives you an idea. So, the collective memory of the Famine and of the people forced to flee their homes is something that I think must always resonate profoundly in Irish Society.

As a country, we have known what it is to be hungry and to be forced to flee our homes. And it isn't only that because new research is showing, particularly the excellent work at University College Cork on the famine, that many people died on their way to the port. And to actually pay the fare of £3.10 to go to Canada or £5 to go to an American port required that you had something to sell, a cow perhaps or the last implements or whatever. But many died and it is the reason why there is a gap in the figures. Again, in relation to others, we have details of where people die but not where they were baptised because they died on the way and so forth.

I think that this memory of our past has shaped and has continued to shape our values and our sensibilities today, instilling in us a moral calling to help others in need.

I interject here to say that this is not easy, because there is often a contradiction between the ethical implementation of that identification with human need and another kind of individualistic, in parts, to want to be among the smartest very often and to be, if you like, the most successful in a highly individual version of economy and society—a point to which I'll come. They are not necessarily contradictory, but they post a moral dilemma and they impose choices at times.

I think today, millions of people around the world of course face the same fear, suffering and desperation as before in increasing numbers and worse circumstances.

And I want to suggest that the current status being accorded to asylum-seekers in administrative systems and in the media discourse urgently calls into question political philosophies, and tests the principles according to which our contemporary liberal democracies have been drawing the line between, for example, the rights of citizens and those of prospective citizens. After all, I'm in a university with a distinguished law school. This is an argument I remember which we've had in Ireland of course.

We have become accustomed to narratives of how men and women throughout our world, as refugees, find themselves living for extended periods of time in unsuitable accommodation, confined to forced idleness, without even control over their daily diet, so then—as Eugene Quinn, Director of the Jesuit Refugee Service Ireland, remarked—children grow up "without the memory of their parents cooking a family meal." I know things are being attempted at improvement, but I read Eugene Quinn's remarks with familiarity at having seen it happen in too many places in the world.

The migratory experience is a journey of special vulnerability imposed on top of existing vulnerabilities. I am minded to recall the reflections of Hannah Arendt in her 1943 essay, "We Refugees," and later expanded upon in her seminal book, *The Origins of Totalitarianism.* I think those reflections of Hannah Arendt have lost none of their accuracy or potency.

If I had a word that I wanted to see as a major and minor success out of the different papers that I have been giving recently, I think it is of suggesting the difference that there is when people use words like internationalism or interdependency. The dominant time, people will say this to you as people meet Presidents, including myself, that are talking about trade. But really, wouldn't it be a different place if people opened the conversation with people about the whole question of interdependent vulnerabilities? We opened the conversation on vulnerability on, as indeed that fine work of Ian Gough and others, which in his book *Heat, Greed and Human Need* that opened on human need and then it went on to structures. But the notion about it is in fact that it nearly always begins with trade, and I will come later to suggest that—and I have no hesitation in saying it—this has devalued everything really in relation to intellectual life, and it has devalued diplomacy very seriously.

Arendt described the fate of refugees as that of human beings who, unprotected by any specific political convention, suffer from the plight of being unrecognised by the state. In a couple of weeks' time, I will visit and see this in action in places like Lebanon.

She identifies that deadlock that arises from the entanglement between the rights of humans and those of the citizen: in the nation-state, the so-called 'inalienable' rights of man cease to be protected as soon as they are decoupled from the rights of the citizens of a state, leading to this tragic paradox that the refugee, as the one most empirically the most vulnerable, who should have embodied the rights of humans par excellence, represents instead the object that constitutes the radical crisis of this concept.

Arendt has intrigued me because I have used her work quite a lot in recent years in relation to memory and forgiveness. But she, a refugee herself from Germany who went through an internment camp in France before seeking asylum in the United States, had a profound understanding of how the loss of citizenship was akin to a loss of human status. For not only do refugees lose their homes—that is, "the entire social structure into which they were born and in which they established for themselves a distinct place in the world"—they also lose the political framework in which they had "the right to have rights."

Indeed, refugees and asylum-seekers in some instances have been allowed or sustained in terms of both life and liberty, but yet, they are deprived of the context in which their actions, their opinions, their ability to participate in speech (and, thus, in politics) have meaning. For Arendt, therefore, to be stripped of citizenship is to be stripped of words, to fall to a state of utter vulnerability with avenues of participation closed off, new futures disallowed.

It is for this reason, that I believe it is my responsibility, as President of Ireland, to encourage us Irish at home and abroad to be exemplary in reaching out to those who find themselves seeking shelter and succour on our shores. In June, Sabina and I had the opportunity of welcoming refugees and asylum-seekers as well as those on the front line of working with them to Áras an Uachtaráin.

The group who came to be with us that day included families who had arrived in Ireland at different times over the past forty years from Iran, Sudan, Syria and Vietnam. Each of them had made enormous sacrifices, leaving family behind, taking risks to leave their homeland in order to create new and better lives that have undoubtedly resulted in making valuable contributions to our modern and inclusive society. They have brought to us a rich story and experience to add to ours that should never be forgotten.

I suppose to ask you as often you read and hear about it; why is it that all these migratory activity in a migratory planet is always described as the problem of migration? The problem? What about the 10-12% of GDP globally produced by migrants. Why do you use language the "problem of" and so?

Many of the families to which I made reference that Sabina and I have had the opportunity to meet with and visit in recent times are refugees and asylum-seekers moving through Ireland's refugee and asylum system, which is grounded, of course, in the 1951 Refugee Convention and its 1967 Protocol. It is worth recalling the background to this international legal framework.

If we consider the aftermath of World War II as having launched the first truly global refugee crisis in contemporary times, so too did this period and these events elicit an equally global response.

Recognising the urgent need to help millions of Europeans who had fled or lost their homes, the office of the United Nations High Commissioner for Refugees (UNHCR) was established in 1950 with a three-year mandate.

I think it is very well borne in mind what stood behind that decision. Today, the organisation continues to work hard to protect and assist refugees around the world. Underpinning its work is the 1951 Refugee Convention, which defines the term 'refugee' and outlines the rights of the displaced, as well as the legal obligations of States to protect them. And Ireland is one of the 145 states to have ratified the Convention, and several regional responses have since yielded further Declarations regarding asylum.

Now, seventy years after the mass displacement of what was the Second World War, forced displacement and migration are again at record levels. In June of this year, the UN Refugee Agency produced the shocking statistic that the number of people fleeing war, persecution and conflict had exceeded 70 million globally last year—the highest number in the UNHCR's history with 2.3 million more than the previous year—highlighting the growing scale of the challenge. The vast majority are displaced within their own countries; however, almost 26 million people crossed international borders in search of international protection in 2018.

But, isn't it important to just question the scholarship that refuses to look at the structure of the sources of migratory movements? We can have the academic thing to a point of what is voluntary/ involuntary at most. Furthermore, looking at the current geopolitical landscape, it is hard to imagine a situation in which the number of people in need of international protection will decline in the short term. Conflict and instability is now the single biggest driver of refugee flows, and conflict zones have produced the largest proportion of deep endemic global poverty.

The war in Syria alone has resulted in over 6.7 million refugees in the region, while another 6.2 million people are displaced within Syria. Bangladesh continues to host almost one million Rohingya refugees from Myanmar. Over 300,000 people have fled insecurity and violence in Central America, while 4 million people have fled Venezuela since 2014. And in the majority of cases, I say it slowly, neighbouring countries have opened their borders to those fleeing, demonstrating compassion and empathy to the new arrivals.

What is our obligation then to those who do that? It is a very serious one. There are, however, new challenges that are forcing people from their homes. Part of the growing challenge is linked to a changing climate. Dangerous shifts in climate are placing stress on communities, where ecosystems can no longer support populations, leading to a lack of resources and contributing to conflict and violence.

The anthropology of Africa will show you people moving, in many cases creating huge new conflict in relation to pastures and in relation to access to water. And unless we collectively take action to prevent catastrophic climate change, as well as assist communities to prepare for, and adapt to, changing climates, these population flows driven by climate shifts are only going to increase. They are increasing. A lack of development, failures of governance, and increasing inequality within and between countries are also fuelling instability and conflict. This is a deepening, if you like, of what I call the intersecting crisis of ecology, economy, and society. These points are made very well, inter alia, in Pope Francis's encyclical, *Laudato Sí.*

Worryingly, today, the welcome and support shown to European refugees following the Second World War, that was manifested in the 1951 Convention and its Protocol, is somewhat contradicted, to put it most politely, and is under immense strain.

The international system of protection for refugees is coming under pressure on a number of fronts. As I mentioned, the numbers are shocking and challenging, in terms of human suffering of all, but they are not necessarily unmanageable. Indeed, eighty percent of refugees are hosted in countries neighbouring their countries of origin, often without much fanfare or acknowledgement. Refugees, when asked, actually always up near the top choices they would love to return home, and, therefore, you have a whole series of strategies chosen in relation to make as to what is transitional: what is transitional for return, transitional for adaptation and transitional for movement.

However, what I believe is more worrying is the increasing lack of international solidarity, both with refugees themselves and with those communities and countries that host them. This is most apparent in the response to the relatively small numbers of refugees reaching our borders, which has brought forth a type of narrative about the 'other' that we, in the humanitarian tradition, had hoped was assigned to the chronicles of the past.

Countries whose citizens have often benefited from international asylum and migratory flows are reneging on their commitments with the aim of discouraging or inhibiting refugees from seeking the international protection to which they are entitled under the 1951 Convention and Protocol. Pope Francis's injunction that to all this we must not remain mute in what he called "*a culture of indifference*" is one that I so strongly support.

In his briefing to the UN Security Council last April, the UN High Commissioner for Refugees, Filippo Grandi, spoke of the growing hostility towards people on the move. Reflecting on his over thirty-five year career, he remarked:

"I have never seen such toxicity, such poison, in the language of politics, in the media, in social media and even in everyday discussions and conversations around this issue. This toxicity often focuses, sadly, tragically, on refugees, migrants and foreigners. That should be of concern to us all."

And that is the great problem that we have, that we have sunk to this level, or that we have tolerated the sinking of those in authority to use language like this. I fully agree with Filippo Grandi's comments. Regrettably, we are losing, be it through a consciousness rendered mute, broken, weary, alienated, anomic, and, at times, perhaps obsessed with the very struggle for survival in a world that uses one's life but does not respect it, that what is lost is one of the most fundamental tenets of our humanity: giving help to those in need.

It may be the case that refugees turn to their fellow global citizens for protection and shelter, with the hope of a better future and increased opportunities for themselves and their families. There is a bit of a gloss on this I feel, however. The truth is that many are seeking to escape from circumstances where hope has been lost. It isn't an easy decision to leave that with which you have been intimate, the place which you have called home. And many, like our ancestors in their day, have undertaken arduous journeys and, on arrival, have to grapple with a foreign language, a different climate, and a new set of social and cultural customs. They desire nothing more than to contribute fully in their adopted homes. Yet, for many, after reaching safety, they are subjected to prejudice and, above all, stereotyping born of ignorance and fear with the new capacities for communication being used by carrying that ignorance and fear. When such prejudice is driven by political populism and lazy opportunism, it is all-the-more despicable and deplorable.

However, rising inequality is undoubtedly a factor in this increased hostility.

Europe, for example, was a leader in championing the rights of refugees for many decades and, since 2008, it has processed over 6 million asylum applications. Now confronted by the rise of populist political ideologies, of what is not a nationalism but a neo-nationalism, for it does not speak now of any emancipatory tendency towards freedom, it speaks of a calling up and exploiting of fear, division and exclusion—with the excluded often being those who, by their marginalisation, have been abandoned to become the prey of xenophobes and racists.

And while this presents a major threat to European solidarity, it also is a challenge, an invitation, to all of us to stand our ground against such tendencies. As High Commissioner Grandi said recently, only if Europe is strong and united will Europeans be able to deal with refugee and migration issues in a principled, practical, ethical, and effective manner.

In Ireland, we may have, to date, been spared the worst of the populism and hatred seen elsewhere. But we are not immune from it. With that attitude which targets and scapegoats minorities, including refugees and migrants. Political leaders have, in general in Ireland, behaved in a responsible and ethical way. Nonetheless, I believe we must remain constantly vigilant to the threat of these menaces, and the ease with which such toxicity can lodge itself through social media, for example.

As President of Ireland, I have offered an apology on behalf of the people of Ireland when there have been incidents of callous and unacceptable behaviour directed at refugees. I believe that we cannot and must not remain silent in the face of such attacks on refugees and migrants. And thus, Ireland will continue to stand with refugees both at home and abroad. We are all on our shared vulnerable planet challenged to give authentic meaning too to what we mean by those concepts in all the religions of the world—hospitality and solidarity.

In 1998, Ireland was one of the first countries in Europe to establish a resettlement programme. Between 2000 and 2016, almost two thousand refugees from thirty nationalities resettled in Ireland. More recently, in response to the war in Syria, Ireland has agreed to welcome four thousand refugees under its resettlement and relocation programmes. Ireland has developed a Community Sponsorship Programme, on which so much new work has to be done, a model which allows communities to come together and offer to host refugees arriving to be resettled in Ireland. And this is a model, as I said, which needs further work, that has to be resourced and developed to be the receiving, hospitable migrant and community adapting institution it is called upon to be. We need to continually review and improve on our process and our policies.

On the international level, Ireland was proud to co-facilitate, with Jordan, the New York Declaration for Refugees and Migrants, adopted unanimously by all UN member states. It represented an acknowledgement by the international community that there is a pressing need for a comprehensive approach to human mobility, and that protection of refugees is a shared international responsibility requiring enhanced global cooperation on migration.

The New York Declaration laid the groundwork for the development of the Global Compacts on Migration and Refugees subsequently adopted by the international community. Ireland also will continue to strongly support the work of UNHCR and will continue to offer €16.5 million to the organisation in 2019.

The United Nations has the potential to play a transformative role in tackling these issues. The 2030 Agenda for Sustainable Development recognises, for the first time, the contribution of migration to sustainable development. Some 11 of the 17 Sustainable Development Goals contain targets and indicators that are relevant to migration or mobility. The Agenda's core principle is to "leave no one behind," including migrants. And let me now say as a sociologist, and someone who writes occasionally about economics, that this phrase to "leave no one behind" needs very serious revision. I simply put it directly, does this mean inviting those who are not yet participants in the paradigm that is failing to become part of it? Or is an invitation to them to become part of the new paradigm, leaving no one behind in society that has made the planet to the edge of precipice with over consumption and irresponsibility. It is a phrase that I use because it is in the discourse, but to make it critical, leaving no one behind. I spoke with New York University about how you can extract and abuse metrics in relation to global poverty by saying that we are winning the war against global poverty. We are not, but we are abusing metrics to suggest that we are.

This is a good transition to maybe the toughest point of what I have to say: public intellectuals and academics have a crucial role to play, I believe, in giving support and weight as we wrestle with humanitarian crises. They can play a critical role in altering the discourse on humanitarian crises, a discourse that has far too frequently become soured by a hateful, oppositional rhetoric. Public intellectuals are uniquely placed to reveal the structural resources that contribute to humanitarian crises. That, as we would say in the old literature on migration, creates the push.

I have already stated that it is hard to overstate the importance of universities as communities of learning, disputation and personal and social development. However, the present day finds academics and other intellectuals in the public space highly challenged, their very raison d'être I suggest is contested.

Some public intellectuals have been seduced by the reliance on corporate power; other academics, I suggest, have drifted into a cosy consensus that accepts the failed paradigm of society and economy as the only model we have, or might have, of operating internationally. They continue working with curricula that fail to offer, or seek to recover, the possibility of alternative futures, alternatives in the social sciences, for example, culture and philosophy. Universities are challenged in an urgent way by the questions that are now posed, questions that are, after all, existential, that are of survival of the biosphere, of deepening inequality, of a resile to the language of hate, war, fear, and the very use of said science and technology yet again for warfare rather than serving humanity.

And one has to think about it as well. What is taught in economics 101 all over North America? How much of it is real political economy? Or how much moral content is in it? How much of it is game theory in relation to learning riddles that will prepare you for speculation in a further life? These moral questions are beyond ones that might be considered any narrow adjustment in the needs of a narrow hegemonic utility. There is a real concern now that the emphasis on funding from beyond the State has had a distorting effect on the career structure of young scholars in particular, so many of whom now constitute what is really a precariat in institutions struggling under the yoke of a Neo-utilitarianism that is bad for scholarship, bad for society, that has not merely failed, but has contradicted the principles of the UN Charter, and yet so many are drifting through indifference to a human disaster unparalleled in its consequences.

I believe public intellectuals have an ethical obligation as an educated elite to take a stand against the increasingly aggressive orthodoxies and discourse of the marketplace that have permeated all aspects of life, including within academia. Is it not as important to experience the development of the self with others and one's connection and theirs to a shared citizenship and history as it is to become a useful, individualised consuming unit in a consuming culture? Universities, after all, function within a culture, and how they negotiate that relationship, these balances, defines their ethos and output, and it is how they should be judged.

The role of academics, and particularly those involved in the public sphere, it could be argued, is to seize moments and have the courage to provide reaction, to be subversive of received thought assumptions and fallacies. According to the late Edward Said, an intellectual's mission in life is to advance human freedom and knowledge. This mission often means standing outside of society and its institutions and actively disturbing the status quo. And isn't it interesting how the cultural sphere does this so well in ways that sometimes academia does not? Yet, it also involves placing a strong emphasis on intellectual rigour and, if you like, ideas, while ensuring that governing authorities and international intermediary organisations are well-resourced. As Immanuel Kant put it, *"Thoughts without content are empty, intuitions without concepts are blind."*

As I say this, I realise again the precarity of those young (and not-so-young) scholars who, without security, tenure or protection, are struggling to live within a system that, far from realising their intellectual and moral potential, is a source of alienation, allowing a limited distorted resonance with the joy and agony of life as it is lived. Academics all over the world should weep for the destruction of the concept of the university that has occurred in so many places, which has led to little less than the degradation of learning.

Issues relating to the role of the public intellectual have an acute meaning in the context of the United Nations, where I have been last week, and particularly for multilateralism, which is so much under attack just now. The United Nations faces ongoing questions regarding its representation (who should hold power within the UN?), its mandate (what should be the UN's responsibilities?), and its effectiveness (how should the UN be organised and run?). Multilateralism is at a crossroads.

There are, I believe, at least three critical elements to the role of public intellectualism both rational and intuitive: knowledge, ability, and moral courage. And that includes the willingness to awaken society for a noble cause or purpose. In the words of Albert Einstein: *"The world is a dangerous place, not because of those who do evil, but because of those who look on and do nothing."*

The fundamental purpose of the United Nations is, surely all must agree, to ensure that the world does not "look on and do nothing" in times of the threatening rhetoric of war, humanitarian crises, and human rights violations, and to ensure that peace, so hard won, is lasting and stable. And above all that, our words on climate change are turned into action.

We are, however, I repeat, living in a time when the very purpose of the UN is being questioned. As an institution, it is being undermined overtly and covertly.

The wider context in which the UN has to function is one of a trade-driven globalisation that eschews any ethical responsibility, that has seriously narrowed the normative in diplomacy, and that sustains a hegemonic single model of connection of economy and society, with 'development' in turn being used as a conduit for the disseminated singularity of such connection, a notion that suggests that repeating the mistakes of the North will be sufficient for the future of the more populous South. Our need of a new ethically informed paradigm is acute. Our survival, any meaningful response to our interacting crises requires it.

I have been arguing for the exit from a failing paradigm, for a scholarship that facilitates a new paradigm for a connection of ecology, economy, and society and indeed ethics. It is not simply a matter of putting an ecological or social gloss on what we have. We have to strive for a new symmetry between ecology, economy, society, one that respects diversity in all its forms while sharing a consciousness of what we must do together, cooperatively.

I remember those conversations in Central America forty years ago, and Heidi Agorastia and I speaking about civilisation of sufficiency, and of the distinction which you must all recognise in your own life, of when does one make the transition from self-sufficiency to insatiability. It is insatiability that has been the motorcar that has driven us to the point of the precipice.

I believe that quality of life cannot be measured simply in terms of consumption of resources, accumulation and consumption. Instead, we must consider our relationship to, or 'resonance' with, the world, not as we would wish to use or indeed abuse it, but ask how we are taken into that world, how it takes us in and with what joy or pain. In her brilliant recent work, Professor Rosa Hartmut puts it like this: *"from the act of breathing to the adoption of culturally distinct worldviews. All the great crises of modern society—ecological, democratic, psychological—can be understood and analysed in terms of resonance and our broken relationship to the world around us."* Loss of harmony.

Rosa's book, Resonance, is an impressive contribution to contemporary social theory, presenting as it does an alternative view of modernity as the history of a catastrophe of resonance. There is an increasing recognition too in cross-disciplinary work of the importance of resonance, and there is a growing body of evidence that suggests its importance for deep human fulfilment. Professor Hartmut's book is at once a reflection of loss and of efforts towards belonging, as I would put it, having a resonance for and with the world. One can also see how such an approach can reconcile cultural work and the better insights of economic and social studies.

I have elaborated briefly on this concept because I believe this has relevance to humanitarianism and particularly as to the quality of our collective response as peoples to migration. I believe this "catastrophe of resonance" is helpful in seeking to understand the growing narcissism, aggressive individualism, emphasis on insatiable consumption and wealth accumulation, and acceptance of yawning inequality. Reading the popular press, one can see, too, how migration and its consequences is perceived by some as an unwelcome interruption in the lives of some passive consumers, busy about at, the late Zygmunt Bauman put it, being *"consumed on their consumption."*

As a young university teacher appointed at the end of the 1960s, I had myself hopes of the emancipatory power of humanistic social science. We all struggled against the colonisation of what was modernisation theory and we struggled against the Washington Consensus. What I could not have foreseen was the influence of the second coming of the ideas of theorists such as Friedrich Von Hayek, or the influence they would have, not only on theory, but on public policies that would be privileged in the United Kingdom, the United States and elsewhere in the eighties and nineties. And I saw those views from the Graduate School of Chicago, moved from Chile to implement an agenda of imposed market theory and austerity. These were offered not as policies chosen among competing options—the outcome of any inclusive, contested, democratic public discourse—but as a single hegemonic version of the connection between markets, economy and society itself sold to a public as a kind of individualistic natural law as it were, and delivered with an authoritarianism to match as basic needs were adjusted to macro-fiscal abstraction and fiction. Decades of Keynesianism have given way to decades influenced by the theories of those such as Friedrich Von Hayek and Milton Friedman, given way to unrestrained, unregulated market dominance and a communications order with a discourse that 'privileges' aggressive individualism.

All language too could be stolen. I think for example of that wonderful Canadian author who wrote Man's Search for Authenticity. And authenticity became distorted into being constructed like narcissism, when you care for nothing. When authenticity, when it was used by Taylor originally, was one which was achieving fulfilment through others of the self. A prevailing, largely uncontested paradigm has emerged and gained hegemony. That paradigm has had consequences for all institutions including universities and indeed the United Nations.

It is a paradigm that makes assumptions and demands regarding the connection between scholarship, politics, economy, and society—indeed the inter-relationship of societies. In the sense of Foucault, I see it as a kind of colonisation, imprisonment taken into oneself, mind and sensibility.

It has gained strength and encouraged an individualism without social responsibility, within and beyond borders. It not only asserts a rationality for markets but, in policy terms, has delivered laissez-faire markets without regulation. Its colonisation of language itself, distortion of concepts, even emancipatory ones, has assisted in the concept of 'freedom,' for example, being re-defined in a reductionist manner to 'market freedom.'

Consequently, the public world must now become, as it was before in human history, a space of contestation, a space that sets that which is democratic in tension with that which is unaccountable.

As we live through this period of seeking an exit from extreme individualism, a period where the concept of society itself has been questioned and redefined narrowly and pejoratively, when the public space in so many Western countries, the human body itself, has been commodified—and it is when as calculating rational choice maximisers, rather than as citizens, that we have been invited to view our neighbours—we must come together, merging consciousness of ecology, human need, dignity, respect for sources of truth and consolation, reasoned and revealed sources.

We must combine co-operation for that recovery of the public world, informed by the music of the heart as much as by the partial suggestions of ratio. That is what ancient systems from distant places are inviting us to do.

Our existence, in the paradigm from which we must seek exit, is assumed to be, is defined as, competing individual actors, at times neurotic in our insatiable anxieties for consumption. Bauman, whom I have spoken of already, puts it in his book, *Consuming Life, "consumers become the promoters of the commodities they consume."* In essence, therefore, consumers become a commodified entity in their presentation of themselves. The value of humans is debased thus and reduced to their economic worth.

I make this point because behind these transitions lies an intellectual collusion that unfortunately masks a rationalisation. Standing in support of under-regulated markets, of unaccountable, often speculative capital flows, are scholars who frequently invoke the legitimation provided by a university which itself, at times, is put under pressure to demonstrate its utility as the seat of the single hegemonic model of political economy that prevails.

I make this point, because behind these transitions, lies an intellectual collusion, that unfortunately masks a rationalisation. Standing in support of under-regulated markets, of unaccounted, often speculated, capital flows, are scholars that frequently invoke the legitimation fuelled by university. Which itself at times is put under pressure to demonstrate its utility as the seat of the single hegemonic model of political economy that prevails. All of this, as I come to a conclusion, can change.

Universities can lead a new paradigm of engagement with the world, contribute meaningfully to the discourse on the pressing challenges of the day, be it the crisis of democracy, the ecological crisis or the humanitarian crisis.

This paradigm, to come to lodge as alternative in the different forms, necessitates a dialogue that can move out from specialist and esoteric jargon to a broad, vibrant public space that thus retains for the university a capacity to be different, to be relevant once more, to be the source of critical ideas, languages and tropes which can resist the diktats of the marketplace that demand a narrow utility.

And it requires, too, a process of healing, with creative, cultural expression being made possible in public places, and having access to the creativity of the self in interaction with others. All of these issues are about how we look at each other and either avert our gaze or celebrate our vulnerabilities, joys and anxieties in interdependency. We need a new vibrant economic-social, economic literacy, one that can carry merged consciousness from ecological, social, economic, gender activists.

Will universities be allowed to do this? Will they seek the space, the capacity, the community of scholarship necessary to challenge such paradigms of the connection between economy, ecology, society, ethics, democratic discourse and authoritarian imposition as have failed? Or alternatively, will they, drawing on their rich university tradition, at its best, recover moments of disputation and discourse, seek to offer alternatives that propose a democratic, liberating and sustainable future?

I believe that a university response, which is critically open to originality in theory and research, committed to humanistic values in teaching, has a great opportunity to make a global contribution of substance to the great challenges and crises we face; that such a university can be and will be celebrated by future generations as the hub of original, critical thought, and a promoter of its application through new models of interconnection between science, technology, administration and society.

And this will facilitate a better connection between the sciences, humanities and culture, representing a paradigm shift away from the strict divisions that have sometimes impeded academics to realise their best work, and which has perhaps fuelled the decline in interest in the public intellectual.

As subjects are re-cast, unities can be restored, and we should consider Edward Said's suggestion that it is in the interstices between subjects that the most exciting ideas emerge. The change I advocate is about recovering the right to pose important questions such as Immanuel Kant did through the development of his form of transcendental realism in his time: *"What might we know? What should we do? What may we hope?"*

I think these are so important. There is a moral basis to those who are protesting, to those who would like a communitarian new beginning, but, I believe that while fully recognising the insufficient criticism historically by the left of the abuses of statism in relation to personal freedoms, to walk away from the state—which itself has already been deeply ravaged by neoliberalism—would be a tragic error on the part of those who seek an emancipatory transformation in our societies. Of course, to rely entirely on advocacy directed at the state, and to neglect the possibilities and promise of alternatives within civil society, would also be a disastrous choice. But neither is necessary.

As an academic and a writer, I believe in the 'performative' potential of language: words and yes ideas matter—for bonding, bridge-building, mapping out a common space of equal and democratic participation for both sides in conflict. Words are a great gift. They are all the power that some people, and often entire peoples and classes, have.

For some who live and struggle in an unequal world, in areas ravaged by war, natural disasters and political extremism, ideas and words are all they have at their disposal to express their common humanity, their aspirations for what is different, fair, equitable and, above all, emancipatory. They constitute what is for them the realm of hope, as discovered and celebrated in co-operative community.

In combining the tasks of conscientisation with a commitment to original thought and compassionate, emancipatory scholarship and teaching, good intellectual ideas can help bridge the space to that utopia and its praxis that we all, as vulnerable inhabitants of our fragile planet, need.

I think that certainly, may I suggest, the performative, as historically represented in the march, the banners, the meetings, had a transformative capacity that is missing in isolated contexts of individuals, sharing information in front of screens but not collectively experiencing anything. Sharing is so important. I often think about this in one of my unfinished poems about it: *"the night is long and I awake and struggling to recall, the beat of beats behind banners made unholy on Saturdays campaigning"* and so on.

Edward Said, speaking to an audience at the University of Cape Town, involving the example of John Henry Newman, as an argument against specialisation, suggested that the model of academic freedom should be the migrant or the traveller and I'd like to finish with this. We should, Said feels, be free, *"to discover and travel among other selves, other identities, other varieties of the human adventure. But, most essentially, in this joint discovery of self and Other, it is the role of the academy to transform what might be conflict, or contest, or assertion, into reconciliation, mutuality, recognition and creative interaction."*

This spirited defence of the idea of scholar as searcher in pursuit of knowledge and freedom allows for a contrasting of the sort of academic model of the professional who seeks to be "king and potentate," as opposed to the traveller who is dependent not on power but motion. Willing to enter different worlds, to "use different idioms, and understand a variety of disguises, masks, and rhetorics." Above all, the migrant embraces novelty, and eschews predetermined paths, crossing over to the space of the 'other.' This paradigm is the cultural idiom of academic freedom, but it is also the truly liberationist spirit of a genuine republic.

And if, as democratic republics, our nations are truly interested in protecting the republican ideals on which their constitutions are founded, incorporating the founding principles which surely include solidarity, including solidarity beyond borders, then the ability to reach out to others in times of crisis is a key expression of a healthy, genuine republic that is abiding by its founding principles.

I finish by humanitarianism itself. Humanitarianism is an active belief in the intrinsic value of human life. Through the actions of humans undertaking acts of benevolence and providing assistance to other humans, we achieve a form of human welfare betterment.

It is, in its origins, a philosophical belief, but humanitarianism today is often used to describe the thinking and doctrines behind the emergency response to crises such as war, famine and natural disasters. A core tenet of humanitarianism is that people have equal dignity by virtue of their being human based solely on need, without discrimination among recipients.

How much better it would be if the essential elements of what constitutes humanitarianism formed the basis of the discourse that prevails on the streets of the world and within the highest political echelons, rather than those subjects of humanitarian crises being abandoned or indeed targeted as the prey of xenophobes and racists.

And words do matter. I suggest again that public intellectuals have a crucial role to play in their contribution to the humanitarian discourse broadly and, in particular, the language and commentary relating to migration. We have seen in recent times, the souring of language used by elected officials of governments, often those with natives and populist tendencies with regard to the humanitarian crisis, using stereotypes that debase discourse, grounded as it is in irrational but contrived fear and ignorance, provides fertile ground for political extremism and an ideological extremism of individualism at best. And I think it has to be opposed with courage.

I think that in the end, in many cases, we must realise—there is just one other last point I want to make—the necessary requirements of intellectuals I spoke of earlier would sometimes, people suggest, say we are actually working on the problem. And I think, frankly, this alleged suggestion of the exclusive demands of time and effort, of clarity, will in fact be used as a mask. You have in the end to go out to the public world and take on tasks and the challenge of communicating that which you have in fact been the subject of your moral wrestling.

I want to just thank you all, very, very much.

May I suggest that universities have a key role as institutional citizens in fostering a more enlightened and multi-faceted debate about migration. And I congratulate you in providing a 'haven' to international students in addition to persecuted scholars who have been forced to flee. And I do wish to say, I wish to conclude with a message of hope. It would be so easy to fall into the trap of pessimism and become disheartened when faced with the grand scale of what we face, especially in the current geopolitical trajectory.

The concept of utopia is being recovered in intellectual work in so many places—work such as that of Ruth Levitas. But let me only say that which is very important. Ernst Bloch suggested that utopianism not only involves a rejection of what is and what isn't useless, and a hope for an alternative, but also a strategy for its implementation, is central. And I think that is what we must all do in our combined consciousness. Take the power, and the transformative potential of that which is driving the response to ecological crises, deepening inequality, economic crises, loss of cohesion, and as well as that, the grave, grave need to remake the constitutions so that they are enabled to response to the heart of the world, rather than being trapped in producing what are, if you like, hopeless riddles of what is failing.

So I wish you all, what you imagined for the future, may it be blessed in its inclusivity.

Beir Beannacht agus go raibh míle maith agaibh go léir.

And I so wish you success in everything that you do. And I urge you to activism. No matter what you can do, there is nothing that cannot be understood, nothing that cannot be communicated, and there is nothing that cannot be replaced. And it is all there to be gained. And there is great joy in all of that in communal celebration.

Beir Beannacht, many thanks.

—Fordham University Lincoln Center, September 2019

The Trust Deficit in Humanitarian Action

Dr. Jemilah Mahmood

Under-Secretary General for Partnerships
International Federation of Red Cross and Red Crescent Societies

I am standing on the shoulders of giants, since this series has previously brought two of the globe's most important humanitarian diplomats to this stage.

Last April, former President Mary Robinson spoke with passion and urgency about climate justice, an issue to which she has contributed so much, and in October, current President Michael Higgins brought you an equally strong call for action, on the role public intellectuals have to play in defending some of our most life-saving ideas, from humanitarianism itself to refugee protection. I can assure you, like my predecessors, I was partially educated by the Irish and my headmistress, a feisty 90-year-old Sr. Enda Ryan, deserves much credit for my achievements, and is surely very proud of me today.

It is hardly likely that I may ever have the chance to take my turn as President of Ireland, but, like the former esteemed speakers, I am also here with a call to action for you. In other words, no one is walking out of here free of your share of responsibility to help us solve one of the biggest threats currently facing humanitarian action.

The threat I want to talk about is not as obvious as the international community's terrifying failure to take the steps so obviously needed to halt global warming, nor the crazy way that our debates are turning vulnerable migrants and refugees—people who need and deserve our protection—into scapegoats. But it may be just as damaging.

"They never listen, so I don't trust them," a young migrant woman who had spent some time in a transit center in Italy told us.

"You make promises without delivering anything," a community member told us in Beni, in the Democratic Republic of the Congo, the

epicenter of the current Ebola epidemic.

We have a trust problem or deficit in the humanitarian sector, and we all need to fix it.

We in the Red Cross and Red Crescent, are so concerned about this that we devoted a major part of our recent quadrennial International Conference with the States to it. As you can see from the title of my speech, I have an idea about what we can do, and it involves paying the right attention to "going local."

To begin with, I need you to keep these three things in mind:

• First, trust is often seen as something warm and fuzzy. Trust makes us feel safe. It makes us feel comfortable. But the truth is, trust is about taking some risks. It is a leap of faith. This is why it can be lost so quickly. Trust in long-standing institutions is not necessarily eternal. It is also often hard to come by when it is time for fundamental change.

• Second, trust is a matter of life and death. If the right people do not trust humanitarians, we can very literally die, and so can they. On the other hand, if the humanitarian sector (including our donors) cannot find a way to start trusting the right people, then humanitarianism itself may die. Who are those people? Those we hope to help—and also those who want to help in their own communities. This is what I mean by going local.

• Finally, trust is like water. Too little and we die, too much and we drown. We absolutely need trust in the humanitarian sector. But it is not a stand-alone. Prophet Muhammad (peace be upon him) reminded his companions: *"Trust in God, but first tie up your camel."* Former US President, Ronald Reagan, used to say, *"trust, but verify."*

So, trust is about ensuring adequate risk assessment, being accountable, and finding a way to balance and measure both.

This begs the question, how much should we trust?

Setting the Scene

Let me start by setting the scene. Why do I claim that trust is so important to humanitarian action? As President Higgins already told us, humanitarianism is basically an idea—a story we tell ourselves—and stories only work if we "suspend our disbelief."

The historian Yuval Harari has explained that the shift of human beings from small family social units to nations and ideologies gathering millions owes a great deal to our ability to invent and then believe in stories. In other words, having common "imagined realities" that allow us to believe in invisible constructs, such as limited liability companies and nations, as a way of organising ourselves.

Our economy is based on these kinds of helpful fictions. It is only because we all believe in the worth of currency and in the stability of markets that these things continue to function. Over many decades, we have also built up a shared concept of reality for humanitarian action, with a notion that there is such a thing as global solidarity, rules in war, and principles to which humanitarians will abide.

This is closely linked to the history of the International Red Cross and Red Crescent Movement, which I have had the honour and privilege to be a part of over the last four years. Born more than 150 years ago in an Italian battlefield, and now represented through 14 million volunteers in 192 countries around the world, both our individual National Societies and their international components (the IFRC and the ICRC) are among the most trusted "brands" in the world.

But trust doesn't necessarily last forever. We can fall out of love with even the oldest and most traditional imagined realities. Certainly, we have seen many market crashes where that mutual belief, as well as huge amounts of "imagined" money, suddenly went up in a puff of smoke.

Along the same lines, we are currently about ten years (perhaps starting with the Arab Spring) into a febrile period where public belief in many core aspects of "the system" is disappearing around the world. We see unprecedented doubt in government, in multilateral institutions, in the media, in globalisation and trade, and even in science.

About two weeks ago, UN Secretary-General António Guterres called this global wave of mistrust one of the *"four horsemen"* that *"endanger twenty-first-century progress and imperil twenty-first-century possibilities."*

As many of you know, the Edelman Company has been running annual public surveys in several dozen countries on trust issues for the last twenty years, finding a major falloff in public confidence in institutions such as government, large corporations, the media, and even NGOs (though there has been a modest uptick for the latter in the last few years). This year's report shows a continued "trust inequity" gap, with the most highly educated segments of society showing much higher confidence in NGOs, the media, and other institutions than the public at large.

Last year's report specified that only one in five people (educated or not) believed that "the system" was working for them and over seventy percent were ready for change. In the West in particular, the politics of many countries have embraced change of unprecedented scope, with large swathes of voters essentially endorsing Mark Zuckerberg's motto of "moving fast and breaking things," of which we have seen the consequences.

As people reject official sources of information, they are increasingly turning to search engines and social media to inform themselves. In the absence of accepted referees of truth, new imagined realities can easily form in the algorithmic echo chambers, that fly in the face of facts rather than building on them, sometimes based on who is shouting loudest.

Pressure on the Principles

This environment is a new test for the traditional tools of the humanitarian sector. The International Red Cross and Red Crescent, and many other humanitarian actors, have placed a great deal of faith in our humanitarian principles as our central tool for maintaining trust. This is particularly true for the fundamental principle of neutrality. Our statutes describe neutrality as indispensable for "enjoying the confidence at all." For us, this means not only refusing to take sides in war, but also avoiding "controversies of a political, racial, religious or ideological nature."

In his commentary on our Fundamental Principles written over thirty years ago, ICRC legal guru Jean Pictet pointed out that, even then, there was a rising tendency for many to see neutrality as a cop-out, as essentially siding with the status quo, and insisting that everyone must take a stand. He said, *"The Red Cross must make it clear to those concerned that it constitutes an exception, at a time when, throughout the world, things are becoming more and more politicized... The Red Cross cannot compromise itself in this wild turmoil. It has therefore confined itself to fields of action in which there are no such disputes, or at least should not be, and aims at carrying out tasks which rally virtually unanimous support."*

This has always been a hard balance—so hard, in fact, that some of our peers, such as Oxfam, have formally signed off from neutrality. Others interpret it so narrowly that their advocacy messaging stops just short of what one could expect from a political party. But there is a clear price for this. Governments in crisis-affected countries increasingly see humanitarians as the vanguard of political meddling —using crisis situations (when controls are weak) as an opportunity and excuse to push a partisan agenda. In many recent crises, from Sudan to Myanmar, Syria to North Korea, the National Red Cross or Red Crescent Society has found itself the only humanitarian actor allowed access to many of the people most in need. In other countries, like here in the US, the National Society is the only non-governmental actor allowed regular access to major governmental committees on emergency response.

Neutrality is an important reason why. Like trust itself, one does not easily "get neutrality back" once it is set aside.

On the other hand, it is abundantly clear that our current (and potential future) young volunteers are now, more than ever, expecting us to raise our voice, particularly on climate change, for the dignified treatment of vulnerable migrants, for gender justice and inclusivity. To a large extent, the aspects of these issues where we have the most expertise, such as in the human impacts of climate disasters and the humanitarian needs of vulnerable migrants, fit well within Pictet's exception for issues about "which there are no... disputes, or at least should not be." You are starting to hear a louder voice from us on these issues where "there should not be" dispute.

For example, in September, the IFRC released a report on *"The Cost of Doing Nothing,"* which shows that, if we do not change the ongoing rise in global warming, the number of people needing humanitarian aid due to weather-related events is likely to double to 200 million per year by 2050—and that even by 2030, the global humanitarian spend on such events will have already skyrocketed to USD 20 billion per year.

At our quadrennial International Conference in December, we confronted state parties to the Geneva Conventions with a series of scenarios about the rising tolls of humanitarian crises driven by the climate that our members are already struggling to address. We obtained their endorsement of calls to strengthen and modernize disaster laws and policies to account for climate change and to leave no one behind.

Likewise, migration is among the most contested political issues in a significant number of countries. Without taking a stance on whether states should promote more or less migrants, we are speaking up for their dignity and rights, and in particular for their safety and access to essential services. We raised this consistently in the recent development of the Compacts on Migration and on Refugees. At our recent statutory meetings in December, the entire Movement adopted a "Statement on Migration and Our Common Humanity" presented to the state parties to the Geneva Conventions at our International Conference.

We are doing our best to thread the needle between neutrality and standing up, but we know that we will continue to be challenged to do more. Maintaining trust with an activist public (and volunteer) base may come to be directly at odds with maintaining trust with states, yet we need both to do our work.

Rise of the Compliance Culture

As challenging as that may be, solely staying true to our principles will not be enough to maintain trust in the humanitarian sector.

While they disagree on many things, both our individual and governmental donors are worried about value for money, and the possibility that money will be wasted, or even go awry. These concerns are common sense and nothing new. They are absolutely right that this money must be spent transparently, wisely and well.

But the ever-rising level of anxiety about these issues—and the way we balance them against other kinds of risks—is a drag on our ability to save lives.

Just a few years ago, on the occasion of the World Humanitarian Summit, donors and agencies signed a far-reaching "Grand Bargain" with the intention to finally correct some of the longest-standing and most costly absurdities in the way the global system functions. The flame of that moment's courage is still alive, but it is still struggling under heavy headwinds.

On the donor side, these commitments included reducing the "earmarking" of pledges to reduce the top-down rigidity in how we respond to needs, the provision of multi-year funding to allow us to address the long-term issues, particularly in chronic situations, and the reduction of donor reporting burdens.

As of last year, multi-year and unearmarked funding had grown overall in the sector, but only by a few percentage points, according to Development Initiative's Global Humanitarian Assistance Report. At the IFRC, nearly seventy percent of pledges to our 2018 appeals were still earmarked, and less than twenty percent of our pledges overall were for more than one year. We were also required to produce over 1,700 separate donor reports. That is a lot of time that could have been put to much better use.

Trust from the People We Seek to Help

We will do what we must to keep the trust of the individuals and governments that fund us, otherwise money will stop flowing, and people in need will suffer. But what about those people we hope to help? It turns out that their trust is even more important.

Let's take the case of Ebola in the Democratic Republic of the Congo. First announced in August 2018, to date, over three thousand cases have been identified. This is an area suffering from over two decades of conflict, where basic services are already scarce, and people have already been dying from many, less headline-catching diseases from malaria to pneumonia. They do not trust the authorities and they do not trust outsiders. As voiced to Marie-Rosaline Bélizaire, a WHO doctor, people question, *"They say, we are in a war zone. We have been killed—so many people, so many times. So why are you coming now?"*.

Now overlay on this the extreme strangeness of Ebola, with its grisly symptoms, the bizarre spaceman uniforms, the shocking separateness we need from the bodies of loved ones, and the terrors of quarantine. We had already learned many lessons about this from our experience with Ebola in West Africa in 2014-16. Frightened, distrustful people do not seek help when they are sick. They do not report deaths. Some even attack their helpers.

When the virus first appeared in the city of Butembo in DRC, a 25-year old carpenter was exposed to an identified case. Health workers asked him to be tested, to which he responded: *"I had heard many rumours about how those who left for the Ebola treatment centre died... So, I fled the centre and went back home."* When many feel like this, you will never contain an epidemic.

Building on our experience in West Africa, the DRC Red Cross organised volunteers to undertake safe and dignified burials. Hundreds of volunteers regularly collect information from the neighbours and communities about rumours, attitudes, fears and complaints. With help from the Centre for Disease Control (CDC), we analysed this data to get a granular sense of what people were thinking.

In some communities, we heard that people thought that our burial teams were replacing the bodies with rocks and then selling their organs. They thought that people transported to Ebola treatment centres were injected with poison and then died. With our community engagement and accountability programmes, we found ways to address these fears (for instance, by ensuring that family members could see their loved ones being prepared at the time of burial). Taking simple measures, like changing from an opaque to a translucent body bag, does much to dispel doubt and mistrust. Yes, we listened, and more importantly, we acted.

In late October 2018, only 28% of reports of Ebola deaths were coming to the DRC Red Cross from the communities themselves, with the rest coming from the treatment centres. After extensive community-based information and education work, by February 2019, 81% of our calls were coming from the communities. This is an important success, and after twenty thousand burials, we feel we are making a huge difference in containing this disease—a good thing as coronavirus seizes global attention. But we can never be complacent. There have been attacks against the DRC National Society volunteers as recently as last month when two were seriously injured. We have to keep listening.

During my visit to Erbil, Iraq last year, I sat and listened to the lamentations of a group of women from local NGOs. They shared some examples on the lack of ability of international donors and agencies to engage, listen to, understand and trust the views of people. One such example is hard for me to forget; if it wasn't so sad, it would be terribly funny.

A UN agency wanted to work in a community and decided, with obviously little consultation, that rearing egg producing hens would be an effective way to restore livelihoods. There were a few problems. Many in the community had no experience with rearing hens and were unclear what the hens were for. Still, beautiful, fluffy white hens imported from Ukraine, costing probably five times more than the local hens, finally arrived. Within a week, half were slaughtered for meals, and another significant portion were sold off, leaving a suspicious community wondering if humanitarian workers were making money on the side through a hen racketeering business.

Ground Truth Solutions, an NGO with whom we have been partnering, has been surveying aid recipients in crisis settings around the world. In a survey of over seven thousand people in seven countries, it found that many—over seventy percent—were willing to say that they trusted humanitarians. But when they dug deeper, they found them feeling mainly disappointed and disempowered. Seventy-five percent of them said that the aid they received did not meet their needs. This shows that, even if we are saving lives, we are obviously not listening well enough to what people want and need.

But will we trust them?

This brings me to the flip side of this issue: how can we expect the people we serve to trust us, if we are not willing to trust them? The Grand Bargain promised not only some change in this area, but a "revolution" in community participation. We are nowhere near there yet.

It isn't that we do not talk to people affected by crises. We are constantly asking them questions; in big operations with multiple responders, affected communities sometimes get "assessed" over and over again by different agencies. However, we are still not good enough at actually listening. And even when we do listen, we often do not act on what we hear, and worse still, we do not deliver what we promise.

For example, among those who are currently living in Cox's Bazar, Bangladesh, after fleeing Myanmar, we found in 2018 that 43% sold the aid they received on the market. The following year, this number was up to 59%. This is in part an argument for providing cash rather than our stock food and non-food items (another one of our commitments in the Grand Bargain). Giving cash—particularly unconditional cash—is our way of trusting that people are smart enough to address their own most important needs. A great deal of research has been done on this, and it fully supports the case for trust.

This is now widely agreed upon by donors and agencies alike, and the volume of cash programming is rapidly increasing. As of 2018, it was estimated at USD 4.7 billion, with an increasing proportion in the form of cash rather than vouchers (rising from 55% in 2015 to 78% in 2018)—though still only representing 16% of the overall aid spend. Within our own network, the Turkish Red Crescent is currently leading the world's largest cash assistance programme in coordination with the authorities and support from the IFRC and ECHO. The IFRC, along with our network of national societies, delivers 25% of the entire global cash program annually and this figure is rising.

However, while donor agencies have mainly accepted the case for cash, a distrustful electorate and press in some donor markets are still making ominous noises, based on disproven assumptions that recipients are likely to "waste" cash, or that cash is more likely to be the object of fraud.

Still, cash is not a panacea. True community engagement and accountability is about more than just the type of aid we give. It is about our readiness to adapt what we do more generally to the needs of affected people as they themselves see them, and not just respond to our own assumptions. We need to get beyond the suggestion box to real transformation.

Let me give you another example from just across the border. Indigenous communities are the most affected by the many natural hazard-related disasters affecting Canada every year. The Grand Chief of the Prince Albert Grand Council in Saskatchewan, which represents 22 indigenous communities, said that for a long time the communities he represents did not trust the Canadian Red Cross because they perceived it as an arm of the government, with whom they had historical grievances.

However, all this changed when the Prince Albert area was affected by severe flooding a few years ago. Many indigenous communities disagreed with the evacuation plans proposed by the government and, therefore, evacuated on their own to a different area than the one designated by the government. The Canadian Red Cross still provided those communities with cash assistance and other support, even if they were not officially registered with the government. This was a turning point for the Grand Chief, where he saw that the Canadian Red Cross was willing to meet them on their terms, even if the government was not.

Since then, the Prince Albert Grand Council has signed a historical agreement with the Canadian Red Cross through which communities will be able to participate in and work in the planning of evacuations. *"We recognize that communities know their communities best,"* said Cindy Fuchs, Vice President of the Canadian Red Cross in Saskatchewan.

In major emergencies, however, we are still often on autopilot, copying and pasting from one plan to another, without taking the time up front to engage. Like many of our partners, we are trying hard to break out of this pattern. In December, we formally adopted a harmonized and ambitious approach to community and accountability that will apply across our Red Cross Red Crescent Movement.

Donors need to help the humanitarian community to succeed with this. This means finding ways to allow for more flexibility in midstream changes of plan. Aid organisations need to be able to go beyond rigid log frames but to be able to listen, adjust, deliver impact, and learn. With all the best intentions, efforts to do this are often still too difficult to be effective.

Building Trust with Local Civil Society and Governments

Finally, we need to address our trust gap between international and local responders. When we were preparing the World Humanitarian Summit (as I was leading the WHS Secretariat before joining the Red Cross), we carried out what I believe is the largest and most diverse consultation ever, about the global humanitarian system. We connected with over 23,000 people, in 151 countries. Throughout the consultations, we consistently heard the message that the international humanitarian community essentially needed to wake up to the enormous capacity of governments and civil society in states impacted by crises—particularly in situations of non-conflict disasters, where we expect all to be pulling in the same direction.

Around the same time, the UN Secretary-General's High Level Panel on Humanitarian Financing concluded that much greater investment in local responders would be absolutely indispensable in a world where humanitarian needs continue to far outpace international funding (to the tune of over USD 15 billion) and where global appeals are constantly under-funded (usually persistently around 60%). The rationale for investment in local actors was certainly related to value for money, including over the long term, but touched on other values as well. Local actors can work much more efficiently in response to emergencies, and investments in them build sustainability by connecting today's response with tomorrow's preparedness capacity. Increasing focus on "localisation" was one of only a handful of game-changing steps the Panel recommended to bridge the humanitarian financing gap over the long term.

Local actors also bring advantages when it comes to winning the community's trust. As pointed out in the Edelman Trust Barometer, "people in my community" were among the most trusted categories of persons in 2020 and "people like myself" were considered among the most credible sources of information. With this in mind, community-level volunteers, like those supporting National Red Cross and Red Crescent Societies, have some of the best chances of winning the trust of affected persons in their communities, as we have seen in the DRC Ebola virus example.

Many international NGOs and UN agencies have realised this and look to directly hire as many local staff as possible. Unfortunately, particularly in a major and protracted response operation, this can have the reverse effect of undermining local capacity, because talented governmental and local civil society staffers are lured away by better-paid positions, leaving their local institutions and organisations weaker. This is not the way to strengthen local capacity.

There are still major hurdles to overcome. Overall, direct funding to local actors (the majority of it to governments and not civil society) has barely budged—from 2.0% (USD 433 million) of overall humanitarian funding in 2016 to 3.1% (USD 648 million) in 2018, while less direct funding was estimated that year at 8.74%. Most of the funds they received were through intermediaries, such as UN agencies or INGOs, with consequent added expense, as well as loss of direct communication and understanding—between those carrying out the work at the last mile and those paying for it.

Local actors complained that they were often treated as sub-contractors, with little discretion to make use of their knowledge of local needs and traditions, and very little opportunity to obtain support for their long-term capacity.

This led to a commitment in the Grand Bargain to increase funding channelled to national and local responders "as directly as possible" (removing multiple layers) to 25% of the overall humanitarian spend by 2020, as well as to increase investment in their institutional capacity, support their voices in coordination mechanisms, and promote stronger partnerships between international and local responders. None of these goals could be met without significant levels of trust between international and local partners.

Together with the Swiss Government, the IFRC has acted as a co-convener of the Grand Bargain's Localisation Workstream, where signatories are cooperating to support each other in carrying out their commitments. Since 2016, we have seen important progress on some of those commitments, but much less in others.

Many donors, UN agencies, and INGOs have been rethinking how they work with local partners, changing policies that get in the way, and piloting new approaches. For example, Italy revised procedures in 2016 and moved to a direct funding relationship with its first local NGO partners. The ACT Alliance changed the rules for its Rapid Response Fund to make it available only to local actors. Mercy Corps ran a capacity building program in Syria, through which local partners received remote coaching, mentoring, training, and ongoing support to strengthen their capacity in financial, operational, and programmatic areas. UNHCR changed its policy on providing overhead costs, which had provided INGOs an overhead amount on contracts but not local civil society organisations. Germany and many other donors significantly increased their support for the UN's Country-Based Pooled Funds, with the ambition that many of those funds would increase the number of local actors receiving funding. While this has achieved progress in some contexts, it has not across the board, and still has many challenges for local actors to gain direct benefit.

Apart from IFRC, which is the largest global humanitarian network, others, particularly faith-based network organisations, like Act Alliance and Caritas have long devoted themselves to supporting local actors to respond in their own communities. But we also have many things to improve. Last December, the IFRC general assembly adopted a new ten-year strategy committing themselves to a series of transformations, including a major shift of leadership and decision-making, to the most local level—particularly to our 165,000 branches, where most important services are delivered.

During our visits to several "demonstrator countries" and in regional workshops in Africa, Asia-Pacific, and the Middle East, we heard from many local actors who struggled with repeated capacity assessments and heavy due diligence processes, after which they were still often treated as sub-contractors. Women-led and women's rights organisations report particular difficulties breaking into humanitarian financing and coordination mechanisms.

Donors are leery of risk and worried about the capacity needed to oversee a multitude of new partners. Not all local actors are prepared to act according to humanitarian principles or humanitarian quality standards. International actors worry about how this shift will affect their funding and role in the future. There are still plenty of stumbling blocks on the way to major systemic change.

In the meantime, however, some steps are being taken toward "localisation," whether the international community wants them or not. After the Sulawesi earthquake in Indonesia, the authorities limited the entry of international actors unless they could find a local partner to sponsor them. With the tables turned, and as reported by the Humanitarian Advisory Group, "some international organisations reported radical shifts in their partnership management. Fewer international staff were employed into the partner organisations. In-country partners took strategic and operational decisions... resulting in greater local ownership of the response." The majority of cluster meetings were conducted in Bahasa Indonesia instead of English. International actors were still contributing—but in a different way. As governments grow in capacity and confidence (particularly in Asia), we can expect more to take their cue from Indonesia's experience.

Of course, bans on international humanitarian action are not what we are looking for. International responders will continue to have an important role in a more localised humanitarian system, especially in conflict settings where blocking humanitarian aid is often used as a tool of war. But the turned tables in the Sulawesi case show a glimpse of a response that is much closer to the ideal of "as local as possible, as international as necessary" than many internationals have managed to achieve so far in their own incremental changes to partnerships and coordination mechanisms.

In fact, just last week, my day turned a little brighter reading about SOS Sahel, an international NGO working for more than 36 years in Sudan and Ethiopia, that decided it was time to close down the charity as enough local capacity had been developed to continue the work. We need to learn how they arrived at this point and reflect on the role of many organisations that have persisted for decades without significantly supporting leadership by local actors.

As someone who began her career in the global south, founding a hybrid national–international NGO (or a southern-based INGO as some called us) that somehow fit neither here nor there, but yet seamlessly was able to blend in and learn from all sides, let me also share my personal reflections and regrets.

Local and southern based NGOs have to be very careful not to strive to be a mirror image of the more established northern NGOs. When I founded MERCY Malaysia, I wanted to prove that we were as good as, if not more effective and efficient than, these established organisations. My colleagues and I worked on quality assurance, obtaining the Humanitarian Accountability Partnership certification ahead of many other large INGOs.

All this was very important for our internal learning, quality assurance and commitment to accountability—both to donors and people we serve. I always reminded myself and colleagues that we should never lose what is precious about local southern organisations. As an organisation born in a multi-racial and multi-ethnic country, our humility, our deep knowledge of culture, our innate ability to easily build relationships with diverse communities, our precious asset and natural ability to listen, understand, and learn from the people we aim to support, were crucial building blocks to enable us to deliver the best possible assistance for people and with people. There is no magic formula.

Sometimes, I felt like the token southern organisation representative, this rather unique Muslim woman from the global south, who was a decent communicator, was opinionated and courageous enough to speak out. I am glad there are many like me more visible now, but the reality is we do NOT fully represent all the smaller community organisations, the grassroot organisations run by women, nor the people affected by conflict and crises who can themselves self-organise and act.

So, both international and southern based organisations, especially the ones who are often represented in workshops and meetings around the world, need to be humble and acknowledge that. We all need to do more to build those bridges and relationships with people, and I daresay, to one day be able to allow them to lead us.

Personally, as a result of a more than 20-year persistent and patient journey and stubborn advocacy, dialogues and commitments to localisation are common today. In my lifetime, I have seen the shift we pushed for actually begin to happen.

Looking to the future, I know there will be another hopefully more persistent group of individuals, who will push forward and continually transform the "system" and put trust and power into affected people's hands. And people affected by crises or caught in conflict will raise their voices more frequently and louder. I urge you to read the Guardian article published recently, and appropriately entitled *"Stop ignoring us: Rohingya refugees demand role in running camps."*

In order to achieve this much needed shift, we will require a completely different funding model and system from what we now widely use in the humanitarian sector. The fast-growing application of FinTech, digital social networks, and the ability for people caught in crises to connect directly with those who want to assist, will certainly catalyse this.

It is also the action of individuals, like my friend Amierah who crowdsources funding to get much needed warm blankets for migrants and refugees landing on remote Greek islands. The private sector will increasingly play a role, we just need to know how to harness and guide the partnership, so that our humanitarian principles are preserved. Most importantly, we need to ensure that everything we do will protect the safety and dignity of those we hope to serve. But there are dark clouds looming above us today. A narrowing humanitarian space imposed by governments may enable national and local actors to strengthen preparedness, response, and recovery from disasters arising from natural hazards. That gives us reason to celebrate!

However, closing and limiting access to people caught in conflicts is threatening our ability to reach those most in need and hardest to reach. Added to this, current discourse and increasingly restrictive counter-terrorism legislation can cripple humanitarian action. I would never argue that security is unimportant, but we may yet see the negative repercussion of these regulations, when people feel they are victimised and forgotten.

The Way Forward

So, how do we maintain trust in humanitarian action? Even in our turbulent times, our principles are still a potent tool and certainly one we will want to protect from permanent damage. We hope that this will be possible even as we stand up for humanitarian values when the political sphere becomes so extreme as to place them in jeopardy.

To keep the trust of the public (and through them, our major donors), humanitarian organisations must maintain best-in-class safeguards against fraud and misuse of funds. We must be transparent and conscientious in our use of resources that are entrusted to us on behalf of those in need. And for aid to be effective, donors must also allow us enough breathing space to make some of our own decisions about how to use these funds without being buried in over-reporting and paperwork. To turn around Reagan's phrase—*verify, yes, but with some trust.*

We need to rise to the challenge in trying to maintain trust in an increasingly noisy world. Where confirmation bias of artificial intelligence creates algorithms that drive greater polarisation, where fake news is paradoxically taken more seriously than mainstream news, and where social media becomes the first point of news and information. We need humanitarian actors to diversify skill sets to manage this, to master these digital and media platforms, rather than reacting to them. We need to continually engage in ways that might seem non-traditional today, but will be obsolete in just a few years' time, as the rapid speed of change in digital communication and increasingly available technology to all.

We must work together to go local. This is where you come in. As I hope you remember, this speech is ending with an assignment for you. Going local requires its own leap of faith at a very distrustful time. If we do not take it, we risk losing the confidence of the communities where we work, the people we seek to help, and the governments of affected countries. Losing that confidence can be just as fatal as closing the spigot of humanitarian funding.

What is your role? Some of you, like me, are Grand Bargain signatories. I am sure among you here are international actors and you need to adjust to current and future realities—to be bold, courageous, and adaptable—to foresee what role you are best placed to contribute to, and when you might eventually exit. Others of you are current, and my hope is many of you are future thought leaders for our sector. I need all of your help to overcome that most deadly of threats to change—"humanitarian reform fatigue."

We are moving, very slowly and painfully, toward a more localised approach, where communities are supported to be their own heroes and international support strengthens and enhances, rather than replacing and undermining, local capacity. This is just the moment when many past reforms in our sector have begun to lose steam—when the incremental improvements make the finish line look impossibly far and people begin thinking about the next catchphrase. We need your voices (and your tweets and posts) to encourage all of us to keep on going in this race to truly build a system fit for our future—one that is empowering, and acknowledges that the people we see as being on the receiving end are capable of being innovative, effective, and accountable.

I met someone I admire, Sir Ellen Johnson Sirleaf at the UN General Assembly last year. I lamented how it is sometimes so hard to push for reform, and she replied, "The size of your dreams must always exceed your current capacity to achieve them. If your dreams do not scare you, they are not big enough."

So, to paraphrase John Lennon—*you can say that I'm a dreamer, but I'm not the only one.* I know many of you share the same desire to see not just a better humanitarian system, but, more importantly, better outcomes for people who are caught in some of the worst circumstances merely because they were born in a different place, under different circumstances—not by any choice of their own. We are no better than them if not for that.

If improving our systems and approaches helps us achieve our goals, then let's start by investing in building trust, doing and delivering what we say, with humility and perseverance, to the very people who deserve that trust—the local populations.

—Fordham University Lincoln Center, February 2020

The Sustainable Development Goals and Common Values: A Vital Framework for Humanitarian Action

Vice Admiral Mark Mellett DSM, PhD
Chief of Staff of the Irish Defence Forces

It is a privilege to contribute to the Ireland at Fordham Humanitarian Lecture Series on the theme *"Sustainable Development Goals and Common Values—A Vital Framework for Humanitarian Action."*

There are a number of themes that I would like to develop. These include the importance of collaboration, partnership, innovation, and diversity. I will position these themes in the context of multilateralism, building to my key point which centres on the importance of the *Sustainable Development Goals and Common Values* in providing a Framework for Humanitarian Action.

The Irish Defence Forces are a key component of the security architecture of the Irish Stage, and when all is said and done, they are part of the bedrock that underpins our State's sovereignty, part of the framework that provides for the institutions of our civilised society. For me, a civilised society is built on values, providing a framework for universal human rights.

The right to live in a civilised society is a human right of every man, woman, and child. It is where people are free, where the institutions of state function, and the vulnerable are protected.

I recently read *Almost Human* by Lee Berger. It traces the discovery of the species Homo Naledi, a previously unknown, now extinct, hominin that existed over a quarter of a million years ago. The hominin species predated Homo Sapiens from which we have all descended. It made me think about the principles and values that evolve with civilisation and how they influence how we know right from wrong. More recently, I read *The Jungle Grows Back* by Robert Kagan, which further added to my thoughts on creating a paradigm, a continuum if you like, between the uncivilised and the institutions of a civilised society—between insecurity and security, between peace and the absence of peace.

As a fundamental principle, I see the role of Ireland's Defence Forces is to contribute to an effort to move institutions along the continuum from insecurity to security, from an absence of peace to peace.

Our military is not an end in itself. We are the guarantor of our State's sovereignty and sovereign rights. Sovereign rights that are not upheld are more imaginary than real. Internationally, I see us as a servant, working with others, politicians, diplomats, NGOs, entrepreneurs, lawyers, investors—and always within an appropriate institutional framework, often involving the EU, but nearly always underwritten by the UN.

Four hundred years ago, the English Poet John Donne in *"For whom the Bell Tolls"* wrote, *"No man is an island, entire of itself. Each is a piece of the continent, a part of the main. If a clod be washed away by the sea, Europe is the less."* His words are prophetic when we consider what is happening today.

My sense of his key message is that we are interdependent. Today, in a world of breakneck speed in terms of change and knowledge, when we are physically experiencing the effects of climate breakdown and biodiversity loss, we have never been more interdependent. We are in the era of the Anthropocene—an era in which human activity is the dominant influence on climate and the environment.

Earth's history points to five mass extinction events. When we think of the last two in particular, I think you will agree that the reptiles and dinosaurs were not responsible for their demise; they didn't know they were about to become extinct, and even if they did, they couldn't do anything about it. Humans are different. In the context of animals, we have extraordinary intelligence.

Aristotle marked out this difference reflecting that we are rational animals pursuing knowledge for its own sake. *"We live by art and reasoning,"* he wrote, while Suddendorf suggests humans have radically different possibilities of thinking. So, in my view, if we are to survive as a species, the principle of multilateralism has never been more important. It must become a defining feature for the institutions of a civilised society to flourish. It is essential for human security.

In Europe, notwithstanding the Balkan Wars, we have enjoyed an extraordinary period of peace and security. This security has in no small way been the result of the multilateral manner in which the values and principles of the European Union have been institutionalized, building on the philosophy of Robert Schuman.

But (and this is a point that Kagan makes) the institutions of the EU were facilitated by initiatives such as the Marshall Plan, which, at the time, provided over $15B to support a program for European Recovery—a recovery that was complemented by US interest in Europe for decades to follow. But this is changing, and a new language of unilateralism is emerging.

Ireland is in the top 7% of most peaceful countries, according to the Global Peace Index. We are so fortunate to have civil society, market, and government institutions that are well-grounded. There are many countries, however, where this is not the case, and the gap continues to grow between peace and the absence of peace, between security and insecurity, and between civilised society and uncivilised actions.

For over 60 years, Irish soldiers have served in some of the most challenging theatres in the world. Ireland's approach in providing assistance to victims of armed conflicts and other emergencies is to stress the importance of coherent, complementary and coordinated actions within a multilateral framework.

We emphasise the importance of systematically integrating protection of civilians and gender-based violence initiatives into policy and practice to protect the most vulnerable, especially women and girls. In our assistance programmes, we, in Ireland, also recognise the importance of enhancing resilience by strengthening the capacity of countries, communities, institutions, and individuals to anticipate and adapt to shocks and stresses.

Our women and men, soldiers, sailors, and aircrew have contributed to almost 70,000 individual tours of duty. Our women and men have (and continue to) give leadership, such as that currently by General Maureen O'Brien in Syria and General Michael Beary in Lebanon, previously. We have stood up to violent extremists, and we have freed hostages.

It is in these missions that we come face to face, however, with the simple reality that freedom is *not* free. While on this point, it is appropriate to remember the 87 members of the Defence Forces who have died in the service of international peace, including our soldiers who remain missing in action in Lebanon and the Congo.

In recent years, we have contributed to the rescue of over 23,000 women, men, and children in the Mediterranean, with Irish Naval Service ships recovering over 18,000, many of whom were drowning at the time of recovery. For many of these rescued people, the first semblance of civil society experienced in months, if not years, was that experience on the afterdeck of an Irish sovereign warship under the Irish tricolour—our flag.

But there were many who were not so fortunate. One of our Naval commanders reflected, *"No one was unaffected by what they had to do and what they saw on the mission...Crew members were faced with hundreds of people struggling in front of them [in the water or on sinking vessels] and with having to make a decision rescuing one person, knowing that might mean another might not be pulled to safety."* We have seen hundreds of people die and have recovered many bodies.

According to the Global Peace Index, over the last ten years there has been a general deterioration of global peace and security, and I see further challenges growing.

We currently have two wars on Europe's borders. There is a full-scale hybrid war in Ukraine, where over 10,000 people have died. In Syria, where Irish troops serve with UNDOF, multiple proxy wars are still being prosecuted. It has been reported that over 500,000 people have died, and over 6 million people have been displaced.

There is evidence, notwithstanding reports to the contrary, that remnants of ISIS in Iraq and Syria are consolidating, while others have relocated elsewhere to countries like Libya. Some have linked up with disparate violent extremist groups, influencing further south across the Sahel. There are indications of ISIS consolidating in an arc from Mauritania to Nigeria, encompassing the Boko Haram foothold. This should worry us.

The situation in Mali, where Ireland contributes to both the UN and EU missions, continues to deteriorate. Troops serving with the United Nations Multidimensional Integrated Stabilisation Force have been subjected to many attacks and significant loss of life. There have been multiple atrocities involving civilian communities, about which you are familiar.

Only last Tuesday, three of our soldiers were injured in what appears to be a targeted, improvised, explosive strike. Thankfully, they are well. I spoke to them last Wednesday; their attitude was stoic, wanting to get back to service and doing what they are there for—to facilitate safe and secure environments—just like the almost 600 other Irish soldiers, sailors, and aircrew who serve in peacekeeping and humanitarian operations in 13 countries on 14 missions as I speak.

The porous borders of the Sahel are a challenge in particular in places such as the Tri Border area of Mali, Burkina Faso, and Niger. There is a sense that the insecurity is influencing westward towards the Gulf of Guinea, where the illegal trade in weapons and people trafficking is mixed with narcotics trafficking, fuelling criminality in the region, which spills into Europe and beyond. This insecurity also drives irregular migration, and while we must treat symptoms in places like the Mediterranean, the only hope for a cure is to treat the root causes.

There are other forces driving instability in and between states. For example, state-sponsored cyber and espionage are becoming more prevalent, undermining democratic institutions and threatening critical national infrastructure. The rise in the right is driving more nationalistic tendencies, which, in many cases, is triggered in response to irregular migration, often fuelled by fake news and sometimes reinforced by toxic social media narratives.

I have already mentioned the loss of biodiversity and the impact of climate breakdown—both of which are being exacerbated by the effects of population increase. 200 years ago, there were one billion people in the world. The UN estimates our population will pass ten billion by around 2050. All of this is forcing on and expanding the continuum from where we should be getting more civilised toward greater insecurity and an absence of peace.

There are positives, however, and they are linked to my earlier points relating to human intelligence. Every day, we hear about and increasingly experience the positive impacts from the growth in automation, the growth in robotics, and the acceleration in the growth of technology. These are driving the internet of things, enhancing artificial and augmented intelligence, with the explosion of data presenting huge opportunities. Data drives information, which fuels and feeds the increase and creation of new knowledge and greater understanding. But what does this mean for humanitarian action?

Three things are clear. Firstly, if we leverage the knowledge available—own, open source or partner—and recognise that in every moment, new technologies and new ways of doing things are being created, we reduce risk. Secondly, if we recognise that the rate of increase in creation of new knowledge means that it has a decreasing half-life and we are adaptive to this reality, we reduce risk. Thirdly, the simple reality is that, with such an acceleration in the generation of new technologies and knowledge, it is in our interest to collaborate and partner. That collaboration should take place in a framework of common values and common goals, such as the Sustainable Development Goals. If we do this, we are to make a greater impact in our humanitarian actions.

But there are a number of other features that should characterise or inform the nature of our collaboration and partnerships. We must innovate and create arrangements to support diversity, including diversity and inclusion. This will help ensure a greater impact in humanitarian operations.

Innovation is a systematic change in mindset that permeates entire organisations. Increasingly, the answers to our challenging problems lie outside our organisation boundaries. It is my view that we must be open to ceding power to gain power. We must tame egos and accept that we are increasingly interdependent. Einstein is credited with saying ego equals 1/knowledge. Unfortunately, in my experience, there are too many people who know just enough to have an ego.

Egos often drive the maintenance of silos that undermine better collaboration, trust, efficiency, and effectiveness.

To enhance our capacity for service delivery, including performance in humanitarian and peacekeeping operations in the military, we recognise "opportunities come to pass, not to pause." We need to enable and empower our personnel to act with greater autonomy. We are driving 'Mission Command' that is enabling greater freedom of action for subordinates within a framework of values and in keeping with the commander's intent.

We are increasing risk tolerance, recognising that, while creativity and making mistakes are inseparable twins, mistakes are the portals of discovery. In complex organisations, mistakes are inevitable; what is important is that solid governance for risk mitigation be in place. This requires a culture of learning where lessons are identified leading to that learning, a culture we are endeavouring to make just—a just culture, where there is balanced accountability.

In the context of humanitarian and peacekeeping operations, innovation must also be cross-sectoral, and the potential dividend for humanitarian action is clear. This requires greater alignment between peacekeeping forces and humanitarian NGOs.

The messages articulated by Ramalingam et al. for innovation in international humanitarian action are applicable to every sector contributing to an integrated approach.

Innovation stimulates positive change, providing new ways of delivering assistance to those who need it most. Innovation demands new ways of thinking that challenge the status quo. Instead of being satisfied with incremental improvements in delivery of aid, for example, innovation requires a boldness that continuously asks the question: is there a better way to do this? This may involve a different partnership model, a new process for service delivery, leveraging a new technology, or all three.

Innovation does not happen by accident, it requires leadership, education, collaboration, and understanding. It needs to be raised to a strategic priority. It is not necessarily just about inventing something new, but, rather, it could be about applying something that is proven elsewhere in a new setting. For example, greater leveraging of the '4 Ps' approach, the product or service, the price, the place, and the promotion—how it is communicated has relevance in the context of peacekeeping and humanitarian operations.

Innovation is neither fixed nor linear, with the theory and practice of innovation evolving continually. While it can happen by accident, to be sustainable, it requires a deliberate and proactive shift in understanding, and a culture that leaves us ready to seize those fleeting opportunities.

Open innovation should be supported by effective information sharing, within and between organisations, maintaining networks and ready to codify partnerships with counterparts within and beyond the sector.

States, regional bodies, and indeed the UN itself can encourage sector-wide mechanisms to promote and facilitate innovation for humanitarian action. Safe and appropriate spaces for experimenting and innovating should be stimulated for the humanitarian sector.

Prevention is better than a cure, and treating symptoms alone will not cure the root cause. A focus on innovations can help to support a shift towards proactive work to prevent disasters, rather than only reacting after the event, and towards increasing local ownership of humanitarian activities, enabling a shift from 'catastrophe-first' innovation toward 'vulnerability-first.'

Complementing innovation, we need to strive

1. for diversity in our networks and partnerships and
2. to enhance diversity internally.

Research has linked more diverse leadership with better governance and risk management. It shows a correlation between gender-diverse boards and the increased likelihood of staff adhering to codes of conduct with better communication as well as better financial management.

Humanitarian and peacekeeping efforts are actioned in a comprehensive and integrated manner. In terms of external diversity, we must strive to increase opportunities for external collaboration and partnerships—for instance, seeking to mix state with enterprise and with higher education institutions and civil society actors. In my experience, the greater the diversity in terms of our external networks, the greater the potential in terms of potential disruptive innovative outcomes.

The World [Humanitarian] Summit has reaffirmed the value of convening a diversity of stakeholders to develop solutions to shared problems. Only by harnessing the skills and ideas of a diverse range of stakeholders can we respond to the magnitude of the challenges and implement changes on the scale required.

For many years, I have been on the forefront, advocating for open diverse networks to sense and explore answers to our challenging problems. In some cases, we have created diverse partnerships to seize and exploit these ideas with a view to creating new technologies, with end user solutions to end user identified problems, working with academia, enterprise, and others.

It was such a partnership that enabled our Defence Force's medical teams responding to the Ebola crisis in Sierra Leone to be equipped with cutting edge technology, such as contactless thermometers, before such technology was available on the market. More recently, we have worked with researchers to develop a cellulose-based material for wipes and masks specifically designed to capture microbes such as COVID-19 virus, trapping them inside the material, thereby reducing transmission of the pathogen.

This philosophy is why, in terms of our core profession, we require more holistic perspectives in developing our personnel, not just in traditional military skills, but also as scholars who understand the language of others, and diplomats who can build the alliances necessary to underpin the integrated perspectives and partnerships required for humanitarian action working with others.

I have made the case for diversity in terms of the external partnership, and the same goes for an internal organizational perspective. Spanning external and internal diversity is an appreciation of the importance of science, technology, engineering, and math, or so called STEM. However, in addition to STEM, we must also leverage the arts, encompassing social and political sciences. These define how relationships are formed and how alliances are built.

For us in Defence Forces, this has implications for how we develop our personnel. Whereas, previously, we trained our personnel for scenarios we can predict, now, in a world of complexity, we also educate our personnel for scenarios that we cannot predict. No longer is it sufficient to be a competent soldier warrior; there are other perspectives that are also important. We require a seamless change from being a warrior to a scholar, understanding the perspective of others as a diplomat.

Facilitating 'cross-cutting' structures within our military requires developed diplomatic skills in our personnel to nurture and build collaborative networks. Almost everywhere we operate, we work with partners. Art, encompassing social and political sciences, enhances the knowledge that builds and connects institutions.

In the context of our effectiveness for humanitarian action, we see our drive to enable diversity internally. Developing a diversity and inclusion strategy is critical. Someone once said, *"Diversity is about being invited to the party, inclusion is about being asked to dance."* It is built around culture, creed, ethnicity, gender, sexual orientation, and even age.

Sutton et al. point out how high-performing teams have both visible and invisible diversity characteristics. Visible diversity can enable access to knowledge and networks that are specific to a particular group, whilst invisible diversity can support productivity and problem solving. The effects of diversity are additive for all diversity dimensions. Rather than focusing on one specific aspect of diversity, the goal is to create teams that are diverse across multiple dimensions. "*It is the mix that matters*."

Innovation and diversity are not exclusive. On my Twitter feed, you will see a picture of a young man; his name is Charlie, and he is fifteen and a half. Charlie wrote me a lovely letter full of empathy and caring. He wanted to go to Syria. Charlie wanted to help our soldiers make safe and secure environments for people in dangerous places.

Charlie has special needs, and (in his own words) at times, he is hard to understand. Charlie has helped our Defence Forces understand a broader perspective; he has attended with our troops before their deployment to missions like Syria. Last year, when our values champions received their awards from the President of Ireland, Charlie received a special award also.

Within every organisation—the military in particular—institutionalising a gender perspective, gender equality, and empowerment of women are all capability drivers. Ireland and our Defence Forces have been at the forefront in terms of Women Peace and Security.

I am well aware that gender-based violence, sexual exploitation, and abuse are features of many conflicts. They have been prosecuted as war crimes, crimes against humanity, and, in certain instances, the most grievous of all crimes: the crime of genocide.

One of the strongest indicators of intra and inter state violence is the gender gap. The Global Gender Gap Index is an index designed to measure gender equality. When compared to the Global Peace Index, the results are stark, with a clear and unambiguous relationship between the size of the gender gap and the absence of peace.

I am proud of Ireland's leadership in terms of Women Peace and Security. Our Defence Forces contributed to the production of our three National Action Plans. Within our Forces, we are working hard to institutionalise a gender perspective amongst all our personnel. In a male-dominated organisation, it is as much a male issue as it is a female issue.

I acknowledge that I have much to do to progress our Defence Forces in terms of improving gender balance. I am, however, acutely aware that empowerment of women, gender equality, and closing the gender gap are societal issues which require multifaceted approaches.

The winner of a recent study in an Irish national science competition for pre-university students found that gender stereotyping in 5–7 year-old girls was actually being reinforced by their 5–7 year-old boy peers. This has significant implications, not just in terms of science, technology, engineering, and maths, but also for achieving better gender balance in our militaries.

Better gender balance in our militaries is not a matter of political correctness; it is not just about access to a further 50% of the population. It is not just about being a better reflection of the society we defend, protect, and serve—it is a capability issue, which makes us better at what we do. It enhances our capability in peacekeeping and humanitarian action.

So, I come to the nexus between values, the Sustainable Development Goals and Humanitarian Action.

Progressing along the continuum from insecurity and absence of peace towards sustainable institutions of a civilised society is about striving for common values.

Values are a vital framework for everything we do, and yet, we can take them for granted. Values provide the glue for common action. Values are the bridge between the insecurity and the institutions of civil society, and yet, too often, values are being undermined by seemingly smart people.

Within our Defence Forces in recent years, we have dedicated significant efforts to institutionalising our values in action in everything we do. In a world where power is inverted, where the advent of social media has meant that rapid change and complexity are the norm, it has never been more important that, as leaders, we seek to influence values at every level—international governmental, the regional institutional level, and the state level, as well as organisational and personal levels.

In our Defence Forces, our values include the moral courage to do the right thing; the physical courage to persevere, despite danger and adversity; a respect that treats others as they should be treated; an integrity that encompasses honesty, sincerity, and reliability; a loyalty to State and comrades; and a selflessness which puts duty before ourselves.

From an organisational perspective, values have inward and outward dimensions. Not only do they help make us stronger as organisations, but they also help define how we partner and how we will engage with others. Values are enablers for better innovation and richer diversity. However, values are also about how we adhere to the law—International Humanitarian Law, Law of Armed Conflict, and the Law of War. Values are about ethical practice.

The Law of Armed Conflict, with its principles such as Distinction, Humanity, Proportionality, and Precaution, has a close relationship with and takes its foundation from an ethical basis.

Ethics and the law coalesce to form a necessary combination that is demanded of the conduct of conflict today. Those who do not adhere to legal and ethical standards may find themselves indicted before a court, such as the International Criminal Court.

The Defence Forces incorporate ethics and the law as key enablers to the conduct of our operations, particularly Peace Support Operations. Although Peace Support Operations are not war, it is in a post-conflict atmosphere where the highest ethical and legal standards are necessary. The Peace Support Force must maintain a disciplined and professional approach in operations, all supported by an understanding of ethics. In our case, aligning with our Defence Force's values and with the legal requirements of the Geneva and Hague Conventions is ordinarily expected.

While I have articulated the case for values, my key point is that institutionalising values at an organisational level is a critical component in the context of nested governance, where common values linked to the Sustainable Development Goals drive a vital framework for humanitarian action.

Thirty-one years ago, the Brundtland Commission, in *"Our Common Future,"* was one of the first seminal reflections to advocate for a holistic approach to the key principle of sustainable development. In the context of the norms and principles that underpin good governance and inform our values, sustainable development should be what Axelrod describes as a 'meta-norm,' that is, something for which self-penalisation should occur for non-compliance.

Brundtland also advocated for multilateralism, and corporate social responsibility. There is a clear congruence between Brundtland's findings and the Sustainable Development Goals. The codification of the UN 17 Sustainable Development Goals was co-sponsored by Ireland and Kenya. Attainment of these goals requires governance that is comprehensive and integrated. They represent a universal call to action to end poverty, protect the planet, and ensure that all people enjoy peace and prosperity by 2030. They are fundamental to the framework for humanitarian action.

They address the global challenges we face, including those related to poverty, inequality, climate change, environmental degradation, peace, and justice. The goals are integrated in that action in one area will affect outcomes in others, and the development must balance social, economic, and environmental sustainability. Accordingly, they frame the integrated approach. Innovation, diversity, and values shape how we will leverage these goals.

Ireland is an extraordinary country with a charisma that underpins a reputation for doing good. A reputation that is inextricably linked with values. A reputation that is a driver of multilateralism. A reputation that is a form of power, enabling a small state on the periphery of Europe to play a leadership role on the international stage. A reputation for an empathy that has a resonance from Africa to Afghanistan and beyond to the Philippines and the small island states.

Ireland's values are for a fairer world, a just world, a secure world, and a sustainable world. Our values have been forged in a furnace of famine and migration. Our foreign policy is deeply anchored in the values set out in our constitution. These are also reflected in the Charter of the United Nations, the Universal Declaration of Human Rights, and in the principles which underpin the European Union. This explains Ireland's sustained, strong commitment to multilateralism.

Common values involve a marriage of our strategic intent, as conveyed by the dictates of Irish civil society and our ethical approach to the conduct of operations. They are of relevance in the context of the benchmarks and goals set for us by our membership of the international community and our responsibility to protect, to lead, and to assist our fellow citizens.

We live in an extraordinary time where the rate of change is as if we are at war, and yet, we act as if we are at peace. We are seeing more *unknown* unknowns—'black swan' events—and we now have 'black elephants'—*known* unknowns. I have recently spoken about black rabbits, where our wicked problems collide in a perfect storm of climate change and biodiversity loss, breeding even greater unknowns. There has seldom been a period in our history where values-based leadership was so important. That is why I think the leadership being shown by Ireland in competing for a seat on the Security Council is so important.

Our bid is not about status or power; it is about values and multilateralism.

The American Philosopher Mary Parker Follett said, *"Leadership is not so much about the exercise of power, but about that capacity to create that sense of power in those who are led. The real role of a leader is to create more leaders."*

So, as leaders, we all must do our bit—top down and bottom up—to ensure, for example, the Sustainable Development Goals are being properly codified at the State level and within our organisations. We must ensure our values are codified, actioned, championed, and recognised.

We should all push back where we see cynical populism. We must double our efforts to embrace diversity and inclusion so that society and organisations allow people to be whole and to belong. We must champion gender equality and the empowerment of women, while being alert to stereotyping and shifting the inertia in areas such as science, technology, engineering, maths, and the military. In this, the 20th anniversary of the UN Security Council Resolution (UNSCR) 1325, it is our duty to use all our power to close the gender gap. The gender gap is a driver of violence and insecurity.

Leadership, like innovation, is also about risk-taking and mistakes. Clausewitz said, in war, *"everything is simple, but even the simplest thing is difficult."* In a world of growing complexity, it is inevitable that mistakes will happen, yet mistakes drive learning. I am comforted by the words of George Bernard Shaw, who said a life spent making mistakes is not only more honourable, but more useful than a life doing nothing.

In summary, in a world of complexity, we are increasingly interdependent, and sharing knowledge is critical. Increasing complexity, characterized by wicked problems, growing insecurity, and challenging vectors on one hand, and the explosion in data, knowledge, and understanding on the other, necessitates that we should be collaborating and partnering, rather than isolating. Our collaboration should be characterized by innovation and diversity and be built on values that help to ensure that our understanding is applied with wisdom.

Knowledge and understanding without values leads to populism, unilateralism, and selfishness. Knowledge and understanding in a framework of values leads to multilateralism that drives the potential for wisdom. George Bernard Shaw said, *"We are made wise, not by the recollection of our past, but by our responsibility for our future."*

Progressing along the continuum from the insecurity and absence of peace towards sustainable institutions of a civilised society requires leadership, values-based leadership. Values are inextricably linked to character, and, as leaders, we need to accentuate that character. If we are to ensure the appropriate culture in our organizations, we need a culture we proactively design, rather than one we react to by default.

While I have articulated the case for our values, my key point is that institutionalising values at an organisational level is a critical component in the context of nested governance, where common values linked to the Sustainable Development Goals drive a vital framework for humanitarian action.

It has been said that the eyes of the future are looking back at us, and they are praying that we see beyond our time.

The UN is a remarkable institution, and when all is said and done, it is us. When I think of the UN, I think of John F. Kennedy, who, in a speech to be conveyed in Dallas that tragically was never delivered, reflected: *"We, in this generation, are—by destiny rather than by choice—the watchmen on the walls of world freedom. We ask, therefore, that we may be worthy of our power and responsibility, that we may exercise our strength with wisdom and restraint, and that we may achieve in our time and for all time the ancient vision of 'peace on earth, good will toward men' (and I add women). That must always be our goal, and the righteousness of our cause must always underlie our strength."*

—The Permanent Mission of Ireland to the UN, March 2020

Humanitarian Access

Jamie McGoldrick

Deputy Special Coordinator for the Middle East Peace Process, United Nations Resident and Humanitarian Coordinator

I will present based on operational challenges and less on the legal approaches to interacting with non-state actors and de facto authorities for the purpose of being able to deliver humanitarian assistance to vulnerable people, often caught up in conflict, and in territory not controlled by the legitimate or recognized government. I will focus on Hamas in Gaza and the Houthis in Yemen.

Today, all roads—political, social, economic, and humanitarian—lead to COVID-19. COVID-19 is changing our world, the way we operate, and part of the humanitarian access challenges we face where we work. The COVID-19 pandemic has upended society, bringing the economy to a halt in entire countries and threatening the lives of tens of millions.

In my current position as UN Resident and Humanitarian Coordination on Palestine, COVID-19 has changed the long-standing paralyzed political dynamics, perhaps temporarily or longer.

The non-political nature of the COVID pandemic created—maybe for the first time ever—an imperative for broad cooperation between all sides—Israel, the Palestinian Authority, and Hamas. In other words, the self-interest of all concerned now drives the need to cooperate on containment and distribution of equipment and materials. Even more than the destructive aftermath of the 2014 war, the COVID crisis has opened doors for Israeli facilitation of access to goods, equipment, etc., previously thought unimaginable. So much so, that Israel itself is contributing with in-kind assistance to Gaza.

There are many threats to humanitarian assistance worldwide. The two main challenges are the increased political grip on humanitarian funding and humanitarian access. Reductions in funding globally occur as humanitarian needs grow and are linked increasingly to humanitarian assistance choices based on political considerations and impacted by a growing world disorder. The other biggest obstacle facing humanitarians is access.

In many of the countries where we operate, we cannot deliver food and other things because of political obstacles. For example, during the height of the war, to deliver aid in Syria, agencies cooperated with whatever limits President Assad wanted to impose—that included which agency we could deliver aid through, and where the aid could go. Obviously, aid was not delivered easily into the areas that opposed him. Therefore, it makes it very difficult to deliver aid neutrally, impartially, and independently. We see the same situation in many places where the opposition wants to stop humanitarian agencies from delivering aid.

Humanitarian access is about finding ways to reach people who need assistance. A simple idea, but complex, when control over territory and armed conflict are in play. Non-state actors and governments all try to exert control, influence over the access, the recipients, and the aid itself. In this context, I will address access issues of the newest crises of the Middle East: in Yemen, where I was based before my current position, and in Palestine, which is the oldest humanitarian and political crisis in the region. Both face similar geo-political challenges and similar root causes. Thus, we may find that similar lessons can be drawn to address the challenges.

Engaging with non-state actors and de facto authorities for humanitarians is increasingly important for the majority of conflicts in which humanitarian actors operate. Security incidents affecting aid workers have more than tripled over the past decade, and there is a growing concern over the role non-state actors have in such insecurity. Moreover, when non-state actors control territory, and therefore access to populations, humanitarians have to negotiate access in order to deliver aid. Yet the vast majority of humanitarian agencies fail to engage effectively with non-state actors, and it is the aid workers and those in need of their help who suffer the detrimental consequences of that lack of engagement.

The growing counter terrorism legislation is a recently new emerging threat that affects our work with non-state actors. Countering terrorism, or the "war on terror," is a foreign policy imperative for the United States and most major donors to humanitarian organizations. The onus tends to be on implementing agencies, whether from the U.N. system or individual nongovernmental organizations, to fall in line. The pressure to adhere to these governments' foreign policy agendas is immense. Humanitarians see that this unrecognized consequence of the "war on terror" has its effects on the ability of humanitarian organizations to reach people in need.

Most humanitarian organizations are highly dependent on government funding, which limits their operational independence. They often choose to accept funding with restrictive counter-terror clauses as part of the bargain. After years of global focus on the threat of terrorism, the public and the media are understandably wary of any risk that aid will be diverted from those in need to those affiliated with armed groups. Fear of even the slightest diversion damaging the reputation of the organization creates pressure to accept the premise and the procedures of government-funded aid programs. Especially in the case of Israel and Palestine, there are individuals and advocacy groups prepared to attack the legitimacy of organizations based on real or imagined violations of counter-terror regulations.

We have a clash of cultures—political agendas rubbing up uncomfortably against humanitarian principles. The premise of counter terrorism legislation is that humanitarian agencies do not distinguish between armed actors, including designated terrorist groups, and civilians. In fact, these agencies make every effort to do so to carry out their mission in keeping with humanitarian principles. Far from trying to evade or work around counter-terrorism regulations, humanitarian organizations devote an increasing amount of time and resources to comply with a complex and ever-changing regulatory regime in which they are forced to assume all the risk. Some humanitarian organizations have fallen afoul and been embroiled in costly legal battles over allegations of allowing donor aid to end up in the pockets of non-state actors.

Humanitarian agencies that do engage with non-state actors are often hesitant to admit that they do so, particularly when such groups are labeled as "terrorists"; they are often reluctant to share their experiences with other aid workers or publicly speak about them.

In 2016, the United Nations Secretary-General convened the World Humanitarian Summit in Istanbul. The first-ever summit of this scale, it was set up to identify solutions to today's most pressing challenges in meeting the needs of people affected by conflicts and disasters, and to set an agenda for keeping humanitarian action fit for the future. Over a thousand recommendations later, the Summit is a distant memory, but the problems it set out to address continue to fester.

One important group, however, was missing throughout the consultations leading up to the World Humanitarian Summit—the non-state actors. In that regard, the Summit was a lost opportunity. Clearly these actors couldn't be present. But some more research on the current state of affairs would have been helpful to enrich the conversation around one the biggest challenges humanitarians face today.

Perhaps one of its main successes was the fact that it took place at all. More could have been made of the Summit. The purpose of the Summit was to set an agenda for humanitarian action to collectively address today's most pressing humanitarian challenges. However, non-state actors—which play an integral role in allowing or hindering humanitarian operations in conflicts from Syria, Yemen, and Somalia to Colombia and the Central African Republic—were not part of the consultations in the lead up to the Summit. There wasn't enough work done on the potential impact of counter terrorism legislation and a better understanding of engagement with non-state actors.

All of that said, excellent research and policy work is being carried out by many parts of the humanitarian world including Geneva Call, OCHA Peer to Peer initiative, NGOs such as the Norwegian Refugee Council, as well as the Humanitarian Policy Group of the ODI, and Chatham House International Law Program, to name a few.

In practice, as humanitarians, the range of crises and interventions we are working on are no longer short-term ones. In many cases, some of these current emergencies are long standing and seemingly infinite. Obviously, we face a polarized new world disorder. We face it in Palestine and Yemen—places where I have worked most recently. Humanitarian work is often driven by Member States' political considerations. Our own struggle is politics over humanity, and I think increasingly humanity loses out more often than not.

Palestine

If the Israeli-Palestinian conflict is one of the most intractable of our time, the humanitarian situation it has produced over many years is certainly one of the most complex, protracted, and entrenched. In such a polarised and visceral environment, the line between addressing the long-term humanitarian consequences of conflict—in this case, the cumulative effect of almost half a century of occupation—and being seen to stand in judgment over its causes, can quickly become blurred.

Humanitarian organisations cannot, however, afford to stray across the line into the domain of politicians and peacemakers—at least not if they want to be accepted across the board, with an approach that is credible and relevant. One false step in this minefield—be it an action or words—can set off charges of bias or prejudice, and ultimately stymie humanitarian access to people in urgent need of protection and assistance, whatever side of the frontline they may be on. This is true in armed conflicts around the world, although in Israel and the Occupied Palestinian Territory, where perspectives of national identity, history, politics, and human suffering have become so intertwined, the path of neutrality has been as delicate as it has been crucial.

Yet, "neutrality, independence and impartiality" risks becoming an empty mantra unless the humanitarian response is also seen to be effective.

In Palestine, the humanitarian community tries to prevent any backlash. It's interesting to assess the amount of time we spend as UN agencies and NGOs on fact-checking, devoting equal amounts of time to the Israeli side or the Palestinian side (in reports), and trying to address the complaints that come along all the time, which tie us up in terms of what we do. This has led to self-censoring and a sort of dangerous silence.

Prime Minister Netanyahu has been emboldened by the support he's received from Washington, and that's pushed him very hard to achieve as much as possible, evidenced by the US Embassy move to Jerusalem, the annexation of the Golan, funding cuts to UNRWA, the Palestinian Authority, etc. The recently released Trump plan was wholeheartedly welcomed by the Government of Israel. On paper it is designed to bring massive gains in terms of annexing land for Israel, recognition of illegal settlements, etc., as laid out in the recently published maps of the suggested areas in the West Bank.

The stark, unspoken truth is that the receding prospect of a two-state settlement, accelerated by any move to implement the Trump Plan, will slowly erode the generosity of international donors. As that happens, what will likely remain is a set of programs meekly underwriting what is sometimes misleadingly called economic peace: programs that involve funding for humanitarian purposes, security, and modest economic development, as well as an expectation of Palestinian acquiescence to a continued Israeli occupation.

There are few places as surreal as the OPT when it comes to the issue of humanitarian work and access. Whereas Yemen has diverse and distinct theaters of operation—Sana'a, Aden, Hudaydah—the stark differences between East Jerusalem, the rest of the West Bank, and Gaza require almost entirely separate responses.

The peculiarities of Gaza make it all the more complicated. Gaza is a territory that is controlled by Hamas—a faction that much of the donor community regards as a terrorist organization. From a political perspective, the legitimate authorities are meant to be the Palestinian Authority, who were expelled in a violent takeover in 2007 and, of course, Israel—as occupying power—is legally responsible for the enclave and its two million inhabitants. Some 80% of the population relies on international assistance of some kind and unemployment hovers above 50%. The UN in 2012 wrote a landmark report that Gaza would be unlivable by 2020. And COVID-19 aside, we are here.

It is under a blockade from air and sea by Israel, with heavily controlled and regulated access by land. Energy and water supplies are totally insufficient and the health system teeters on the verge of collapse. In order to get anything inside, you need to ensure the appropriate clearances from the Palestinian Authority, who, despite not being present on the ground, still control the crossing points.

While there is a border with Egypt, humanitarian and international assistance is only allowed through that border under very exceptional circumstances. As a result, our operations require close coordination with all three entities. Easy enough, except that many of the donors also require assurances that their assistance will not benefit Hamas. So with all of this, Gaza is the type of place where the clearances to distribute humanitarian aid take far more time and effort than the actual distribution.

In Gaza, we have Hamas as the de facto authority, the non-state actor. We have a long standing "no contact policy" as Hamas is a declared terrorist organization. Any dealing with Hamas is against the counter-terrorism legislations, hence raising compliance issues. Thus, mainly the UN's political arm, Norway and Switzerland, talk to them. UNRWA has a long-standing relationship in Gaza and the West Bank. Other UN agencies and NGOs are not fully understood by Hamas. This is an awkward work in progress.

The last war in Gaza was in 2014 and resulted in more than 2,000 deaths, some 10,000 injuries, and more than 11,000 destroyed homes—many more damaged along with key infrastructure. The cost of damages was estimated in the billions of dollars. Under established procedures, there was no way a relief effort could have taken place given the massive need for cement and other heavily controlled, or so called "dual-use," materials by Israel.

After the 2014 war, together with the Palestinian Authority and Israel, the UN created a mechanism that would give both governments—neither of them present on the ground by the way—an equal say in what entered and for what purpose. It was called the Gaza Reconstruction Mechanism. It is one of the most intricate arrangements I have seen whereby all concerned goods are assigned to a specific project and then monitored by a team on the ground, to ensure their appropriate use.

At this point, Hamas had no choice but to engage. Most people were not pleased with the Gaza Reconstruction Mechanism. Human rights people said it reinforced the blockade. Private sector and project managers used to dealing with the Israelis directly had to deal with the Palestinian Authority—a government that was not present. In the end, it worked for its intended purpose—reconstruction has been largely completed and could not have happened without this mechanism. Whether it has a purpose or not anymore is a question, especially as the Palestinian Authority has now adopted a largely negative approach to Gaza through a series of overt and more covert sanctions. But with regard to the humanitarian specifically, the mechanism facilitated repairs and construction of water treatment, sewage, and desalination networks, hospitals and health clinics, as well as the entry of items like solar panels to power these installations.

In Gaza, as a result of the tension and volatility we have seen over the past two years since the Great March of Return demonstration, we were never too far away from a repeat of the 2014 war. The UN Special Coordinator for the Middle East has often stated this warning during the past two years in his monthly briefings to the Security Council. Weekly demonstrations at the fence on a Friday have resulted in over 30,000 people injured and almost 8,000 shot, with over 200 dead. There are over 1,500 young people for the most part with lower limb injuries as a result of being shot at the fence. Among the young there is a great deal of despondency and despair over their future. They can see other people their same age on social media pages living a normal life—they crave that. Over the past two years, there have been many occasions where rockets were fired indiscriminately into Israel from Gaza. And there were many incidents of retaliatory airstrikes by Israel Military Forces inside Gaza.

The recent history of Gaza offers a grim warning of the severe consequences that can follow when international assistance declines and is divorced from politics. When Hamas took over Gaza in 2007, the PA split between Hamas-controlled Gaza and the Fatah-controlled West Bank. As two-state diplomacy began to lose traction, international actors simply postponed efforts to address this problem. Some international assistance continued to flow to Gaza, but it was seen as humanitarian support. Politics and mediation are limited currency in the Palestinian context. Direct Palestinian and Israeli talks are frozen. The intra-Palestinian schism is ever widening between Hamas in Gaza and Fatah in Ramallah.

Most donors avoided supporting official institutions and politics more broadly. Attention, diplomatic energy, and funds shifted elsewhere (primarily to the West Bank and the Palestinian Authority there). After more than a decade, the results are clear: disastrous humanitarian conditions, radicalization, and periodic bouts of violence. Rather than an actual peace process, the negotiations that take place between Israelis and Palestinians in Gaza alternate between containing violence and threatening it.

As humanitarians, we meet regularly with the Hamas liaison people, as well as with military intelligence and politicians when there are major issues to resolve. On a more technical and operational level, we work with them on what the non-state actors' obligations are as an authority in a place like Gaza. To do that, the UN created a red line document on what they need to do, and what we need to do. To manage expectations, we have a technical conversation on the things that matter to them, because they want recognition. Hamas wants legitimacy, which we cannot offer, and wants to be treated almost like a government. What we can offer is some sort of regular communication with them. If we do not build trust and enhance mutual understanding, they will block our movements.

We have to listen to Hamas, and listen to their concerns. We also have to seize the opportunity to remind them of their obligations under humanitarian law. This is something on which we have to work on a regular basis. Hamas as a political and military outfit is not fully aware of the humanitarian system, the different organizations, how they operate, and the governance structures. Regardless of the optics, we need to build trust, especially for UN agencies and NGOs who have arrived in Gaza for humanitarian reasons since the early 2000s. UNRWA is a long-standing service provider in Gaza and the West Bank, and has a different status and perception than the newer organizations. It is important that Hamas better understand these changes to improve trust and access.

The current 'no contact policy' of the international community with Hamas hardly makes sense, especially when we see this in light of the mediation and diplomatic outreach and inclusion with the Taliban in Afghanistan. What marks Hamas as different?

With the Palestinian Authority based in Ramallah, recent history has shown they could be more supportive to the needs in Gaza than is the case at the moment, given the overwhelming humanitarian and socio-economic needs there. International donor support for Palestine has been diminishing since 2012. The Palestinian Authority often views the international community as competition given diminishing donor funding, and especially in light of their budget support being reduced as well. The Palestinian Authority has been having difficult discussions with Israel for some time over tax revenue—collected by Israel for the Palestinian Authority—being held back in the amount it deemed the Palestinian Authority distributed as prisoner payments. A significant percentage of the Palestinian Authority's budget is missing from that source as well. It has been a regular occurrence that government salaries do not get paid in full, and services delivery is limited. Recently, and especially in light of the COVID-19 outbreak, the transfer of funds from Israel to the Palestinian Authority has improved with relations being more collaborative.

In terms of the Israeli Government, it is operating via purposeful fragmentation. They deal with us through liaison. They deal with us through the civilian arm of the IDF. We do not see Shin Bet. We do not see military intelligence and others who control everything in terms of movements. This fragmented approach to contact is not optimal to achieve consistent and positive access and movement. This fragmentation suits the Israelis and undermines the humanitarian community's own coherence. We all meet at different levels but our messaging does not necessarily cohere.

We are supported and encouraged by the Government of Israel, because they recognize the importance of humanitarian assistance in Gaza to maintain a modicum of peace. We have a pleasant interface with the technical areas of the Government of Israel who are for the most part willing to facilitate our work in Gaza and the West Bank.

We spend a lot of time pushing back on false allegations created by a well-organized set of Israeli NGOs. Our operational space is reduced by the severe scrutiny from very active Israeli Non-Governmental organizations with links to the government who issue reports and allegations, causing humanitarian organizations to spend a lot of time addressing often unfounded allegations, which is costly. As humanitarians we welcome any type of scrutiny if it leads to a more effective and efficient response. Instead, we use up much needed staff capacity and resources to push back on these allegations.

We're also trying to create a unified humanitarian country team approach with NGOs and UN agencies on International Humanitarian Law violations and demolitions in the West Bank. In addition, we issue regular statements and are available to take on any media on any issue. We try to be consistent and balanced in the words and advocacy we employ.

Again, we have witnessed a different kind of collaboration with the COVID-19 response when the goal of addressing the outbreak, containment, and treatment is a common goal: to defeat "the virus [that] knows no borders and no state can defeat alone." Therefore, the fight against COVID-19 is a global challenge that requires a multilateral approach.

Yemen

Yemen's war has created one of the world's worst humanitarian disasters; between 70 and 80 percent of the population is in need of humanitarian assistance, and over half of its 26 million people face food insecurity. Localised fighting escalated into full-blown war in March 2015 when a Saudi-led coalition intervened on behalf of the internationally recognised government of President Abed Rabbo Mansour Hadi against an alliance of the Houthi militias and fighters aligned with former President Ali Abdullah Saleh. The conflict has fragmented a weak state, destroyed the country's meager infrastructure, and opened vast opportunities for many terrorist affiliated groups to grow and seize territory.

The legitimate Government of Yemen is based outside the country in Riyadh, and has an internal base in Aden, to the south. I was regularly criticized for being silent on the Houthis, and being present in Sana'a, not having our UN Yemen office in Aden in the south. The government was very critical of the way we worked with the Houthis, noting that we "didn't call them out" often enough. The legitimate government was unable or unwilling to comprehend the humanitarian dimension of the international community's role in Yemen.

We tried to meet the recognized Government of Yemen on a regular basis in Aden and in Riyadh. We wrote letters to them, keeping them informed, reminding them of their responsibilities, reinforcing neutrality and impartiality. A couple of times, a PNG threat was in the air for me and some of my colleagues.

The Saudi-led coalition was made up of Saudi Arabia and the Emirates, with support from the UK and the US—curious composites I would say—and the interaction we had with them was not very unified. It was a compromise to take funds from all of these parties, but we did it in a pragmatic way. It was important we took that, but it also reminded them of the obligations they had under international law, and that's been done many times.

Access to Yemen via air, land, and sea was controlled by the Saudi-led coalition. Access for donors and the media became very politicized. Also, humanitarian access inside the country was always a challenge. I would meet them on a regular basis, mostly late at night in the south of Sana'a while they were chewing Qat. We aimed to get them to understand what we were all about and listen respectively to what they were trying to ask us. We did not have to agree, but at least listen with intent. Asking for compliance with the Security Council Resolution meant the end of the Houthis' reign in Sana'a, and was thus a nonstarter. We had to change that whole framing there with them. We also gave them praise for recognizing the security they provided for us inside Sana'a but also inside the whole northern part of the country. I think that was important as well.

I worked with the media regionally and internationally and had monthly press briefings in Sana'a, because the media were blocked from coming to the northern part of Yemen by the Saudi-led coalition. The Sana'a airport was closed to commercial flights, and we were prevented from allowing the media to come in or the message to get out.

I took part in TV panel discussions with the legitimate Yemen Government based in Riyadh to try to counter their complaints against the UN and the space that we had here.

There were no donor representatives in Yemen, and trying to get Member States into Yemen was not easy, but we had low level visits. However, we had weekly virtual humanitarian plus meetings with donors and member states, including those part of the Saudi-led coalition from Riyadh and Amman, including London.

I also visited the key capitals in Europe, the US, and the region to raise humanitarian and protection concerns. Creating a political change within Congress and Parliament in the US and the UK, respectively, was not easy when the crisis was not seen by all as a humanitarian crisis. In many cases, Yemen was closely interwoven in the politics of the region.

As in any context, Yemen and the Houthis were no different in that there had to be more consultation in the context we as humanitarians operate with non-state actors. Research has shown that despite the diversity of non-state actors around, there is a high degree of uniformity in many of the views expressed on a range of issues related to humanitarian action and access. Many of the non-state actors consulted see value in humanitarian action, in broad terms, as alleviating suffering or providing relief to those affected by armed conflict or natural disaster. In the case of the Houthis and Hamas, a way to exert control, to be part of the international effort, is to bring rewards to populations under their control, by appearing to give permission for access and movement of goods to affected areas.

With the Houthis, we established a couple of mechanisms to regulate our contact, maintain the technical nature of our engagement as a humanitarian community, and to get better results. It gave the impression to the Houthis that they had a bigger stake or role in the work we were undertaking. Mechanisms included:

• *The Access Monitoring and Reporting Framework (AMRF)*: a tool for gathering information on the access constraints faced by the UN agencies, INGOs, and NNGOs. It is a very simple online tool. All partners, national and international, feed the information into the AMRF as the only way we can build a comprehensive understanding of what type of issues we are facing, where, by whom, etc., and accordingly provide the foundation for evidence-based advocacy and engagement with the authorities on access issues.

• *Humanitarian Access Working Group (HAWG)*: comprises senior colleagues from different humanitarian organizations. Based on the information from AMRF and the trends analysis, the HAWG is expected to establish some sort of negotiation/engagement strategies at all levels.

• *Establishment of Field Hubs (EFH)*: critical for tackling the issue of movement restrictions at the local level as the best approach to ensure that there is a system for exchanging information and best practices among the organizations operating at the field level.

One of the outcomes of the meeting was a consensus on the need to operationalize a "One Window" mechanism for the humanitarian organizations to engage with the authorities on the different access issues and to bring about more systematic dialogue with the authorities on all the issues raised in the Access Monitoring Framework, which mentioned the paper covering assaults against staff, multiple requests from different agencies, movement restrictions, visas, etc. Very often, non-state actors only refer to assistance; the protection of civilians, or related protection issues, are rarely discussed. In the

Yemen context, each quarter I sent separate letters to the Houthis and to the Legitimate Government outlining and listing protection incidents, trends, etc. The letters were forwarded to all the relevant Embassies, including those in the Saudi-led coalition. Each side only saw the reports of the incidents attributed to them.

Available research has shown that non-state actors see a direct link between the transparency, and confidence in the quality of assistance, on the one hand, and the humanitarian agency's adherence to the principles of neutrality, impartiality, and independence on the other. In the case of Houthis, the motivation was to prevent humanitarian actors from being independent and having free access and movement, based on viewing humanitarian assistance as a purely western endeavor, not in the charitable mode in Islamic culture. This was based on a lack of trust and suspicion of our motives, given that the majority of our funds came from member states that were part of or supported the Saudi-led coalition. Hamas has much more experience in dealing with international actors than the Houthis and have strong allies in the region. With Hamas, they are more assured of their position and don't feel threatened that they might lose control of Gaza. This is not the case with the Houthis who are in an all out struggle. As a result, the Houthis want more control over the work and the movement of humanitarians, and viewed our work through primarily a security threat lens.

Hamas are seeking a degree of respect, and even recognition, from our dealings with them. They have created an outreach within the region. Egypt, Qatar, and one of their leaders regularly meets with leaders in Russia, as well as regional and other Muslim countries. The COVID-19 pandemic might be another opportunity for Hamas to gain even more traction. As humanitarians, we have to be smart and avoid getting embroiled in the political attempts underway to create a division between the West Bank and Gaza. To this end, as the international community, we work through and with the Palestinian Authority in Ramallah when dealing with Gaza.

For the most part non-state actors are broadly familiar with the core humanitarian principles. But on the independence of our assistance, non-state actors suspect that geopolitical concerns, funding, and other factors challenge the ability of humanitarian actors to be independent in practice. With all of the principles, the focus is on observed behavior (rather than, for example, where an agency's funding comes from). Both Hamas and the Houthis know where funding comes from and that it often is ideologically at odds with their situation. But, it is a pragmatic acceptance.

Without understanding why aid workers are or are not attacked, they cannot adequately protect their staff; without understanding why access is denied or facilitated by non-state actors, it is impossible to resolve blockages. We need to better understand non-state actors' views on humanitarian action, including humanitarian access and principles. It would be quite a challenge, but could be immensely beneficial to sit down with Hamas and the Houthis and have a discussion on these policy and legal issues, rather than on operations, including access, movement and security concerns. We often substitute this conversation with training on international humanitarian law and practice. We know that non-state actors, at times, conflate some principles (notably, neutrality and impartiality) and seek to coopt humanitarian aid or otherwise undermine humanitarian principles for their own benefit — much as member states do from time to time.

The widespread lack of knowledge about the rules of IHL governing humanitarian access is a more problematic issue and must be addressed across contexts. It's not enough that non-state actors can rhyme off the core humanitarian principles. This requires sustained dialogue, dissemination, and training to ensure that non-state actors' leaderships and rank and file members understand their obligations concerning access, and implement them in practice.

Hamas is a long established body with the conflict raging for decades, and their regular interaction through line Ministries at the technical level understand how the international humanitarian work functions, the role of the UN, especially UNRWA, donors, and NGOs. It does not mean they agree; however, there are relationships and exposure to the work of humanitarian principles. It does not always result in compliance and access facilitation; often it is disruption and blockages, with humanitarian work viewed as the arm of foreign governments, and based on political considerations. It is hard in Gaza to avoid this opinion, especially the recent cut of all funds to UNRWA, and the politicization of the Palestinian Authority's support to Gaza. But it does not mean that our work is stymied; rather, it is highly regarded and appreciated as it helps the people of Gaza, and that it legitimizes, in a certain way, Hamas's control.

The Houthis have a very limited understanding of the way the international community functions. They have little experience in statecraft and diplomacy. This was the purview of the President Saleh component of the Sana'a Alliance, as the balance of power swung in the Houthis' favor, after Saleh was killed. They were always suspicious of the UN and the international community. Our optics were not helped when the UN returned in mid-2017, and we took over the US Diplomatic Transit Facility, the old Sheraton hotel. In my first encounter with the Houthis Military Intelligence, they stated that I worked for the "United Nations of America." One of the key tasks was to move to a new residential compound for UN staff to live, moving out of the US diplomatic facility. During the preparations for the move to the new compound, and once we left the US compound, the trust between the UN and the Houthis improved.

In several cases, the non-state actors' research has shown that they feel that the humanitarian organizations have not engaged with them in an appropriate, proactive, or impartial manner. In some contexts, engagement is hindered by external political pressures, resulting in serious consequences for aid workers and civilians alike. As in the case with Hamas, some states, including donors, have listed the groups along with other movements as "terrorist groups," which has led some agencies to avoid direct engagement with them for fear of falling afoul of counter-terrorism legislation.

Aid agencies elsewhere fear that engaging with non-state actors could lead to expulsion from areas under government control. These are dilemmas to which there are no easy fixes, and need to be negotiated on the ground. A more flexible and pragmatic, if not discreet, approach from the member states doing the "labeling" as terror organizations would be helpful. The bottom line, however, is that non-engagement or limited, ad hoc engagement with non-state actors ultimately hinders their need for an agreement to comply with International Humanitarian Law. If we avoid contact or engagement, it can be perceived by the non-state actors that humanitarian actors are abandoning our own humanitarian principles and viewed as non-neutral and partisan.

Aid agencies must invest in relationship building with all the parties to armed conflicts and develop strategic engagements with non-state actors. This would be best served, where possible, by the Resident and Humanitarian Coordinator. Under the new reformed Resident Coordinator system, there is a direct reporting line within the UN Secretariat making the position a much more political role. By taking on the responsibility to consult with non-state actors, they help protect those agencies and organizations whose operations could be jeopardized by criticism of meeting non-state actors. But this has to be accepted by the management of the UN and NGOs at the capital level.

There needs to be a level of certainty and commitment from HQs that the Resident and Humanitarian Coordinators will be supported if negative voices and criticism of outreach with non-state actors is brought to the world's attention through criticism in both mainstream and social media. I believe that my attempts to reach out, be it with the Houthis or Hamas, have resulted in more consistent and sustained access. With trust building and conversations being broader in range, we will be able to see more consistency of international humanitarian law in the policies and approaches of non-state actors, and can help serve as a better basis for negotiating humanitarian access.

The non-state actors must witness that humanitarians should behave in ways that demonstrate their neutrality, impartiality, and independence. This must be both obvious and transparent. Any perceptions that humanitarians are not adhering to their principles can have dangerous consequences, ranging from denial of access to attacks on aid workers and their property. This underscores the importance of humanitarians not only behaving in accordance with humanitarian principles, but also carefully monitoring and managing non-state actors' perceptions of them in order to avoid misunderstandings.

This is key to building trust and acceptance between parties to conflicts and securing safe access. It might mean sometimes being proactive in informing the non-state actors before the fact—but not seeking their permission—rather for information. In some cases, it could mean using their technical staff to participate in joint technical assessments to build trust and confidence, without any involvement in deciding the types of interventions, locations, or beneficiaries.

The Houthis did not trust the UN. The UN support was part of the pre-war national dialogue and after that, the Security Council Resolution 2016. Basically, this resolution was to deliver a 6-month quick win to return to normal and reinstall the legitimate government in Sana'a, it did not work. This added to the suspicion of the UN, and it took some time to educate and convince the Houthis that the Security Council was not overseeing our humanitarian work on the ground. Otherwise, it would have basically locked the humanitarians into a position we couldn't move from, and we were then tainted in the eyes of the Houthis. I had to work tirelessly to build trust with them, negotiate access, create red lines in operations, and foster clear understanding on what their obligations were under international law. To do that, I was basically the interface for the country team so their operations were not jeopardized.

Although they have obligations under IHL, non-state actors are not part of legal frameworks and treaties. But, this must not prevent non-state actors from respecting the law, and demonstrating adherence to it. It is important that orientation of leadership takes place and training is offered to lower ranking field staff. It is best to use actual local examples when there have been problems and have discussions around what would be a better way forward to prevent the restrictions of access, interference with aid delivery, etc. Each incident should offer an opportunity to remind the parties of their obligations, reinforce messages, and create inclusion.

It is not an easy conversation to have with non-state actors or de facto authorities. Criticism is not easy to deliver. They seek respect, legitimacy, and even recognition for the way they interact, provide security, safe passage, and engagement. But, one has to be careful to venture into a conversation on non-state actors on their obligations under international law. These can be tricky conversations and need to be thought out tactically when the right time is to discuss. As was the case with both the Houthis and Hamas, they wanted something in writing to help confer acceptance and legitimacy. This could be a simple "red lines" document, or Standard Operating Procedures, with relevant contact points and numbers—without references or signatures.

Finally, the non-state actors consulted in this study often refer to political issues when asked to make recommendations on how to improve humanitarian conditions. Many see humanitarian crises and needs as rooted in conflicts that can ultimately only have a political solution. This is beyond the scope of this survey, but indicative of a shared understanding—across conflicts—of the roots of humanitarian crises and the very political nature of their resolution.

In conclusion, and bringing this back to where I started—with the current COVID-19 outbreak—the international community should explore the possibility of opening up a space for greater cooperation between Gaza and Israel in order to achieve a more effective coordination in response to the COVID-19 crisis. In addition, we should use the crisis as a means to reduce the current tensions between Ramallah and Gaza to avert the risk of impeding rather than facilitating an effective response to the current crisis. In the past week, there have been exchanges with all stakeholders at a technical level, but it is acknowledged that there is a need to extend these discussions to the political level to ensure the right level of response to the growing humanitarian crisis and to provide a base for future development.

—Jerusalem, April 2020

Conflict and Hunger

Dr. Caitriona Dowd
Assistant Professor in Security Studies
Dublin City University

A dhaoine uaisle,

This series has seen no shortage of esteemed speakers issue calls to action and for renewed attention on some of the most pressing challenges our world faces. Today, I want to speak to you about what I consider a defining challenge of humanitarian action in the twenty-first century: conflict-driven food crises.

This is, first and foremost, an urgent moral outrage. For food crises to be on the rise again in an era of global food abundance is morally unacceptable and must be politically unacceptable as well. This is a challenge for which we have no lack of technical responses. Humanitarian organisations have long had the technical capacity to address acute hunger—programme delivery has evolved and advanced over decades to be more targeted, efficient and effective than ever before. As a global community, we have made enormous strides in addressing hunger. What we have failed to address, however, is conflict and its devastating impacts. We do not lack the technical capacity to get to zero hunger, we lack the political will to prevent and resolve the conflicts that drive it.

Conflict-driven food crises are also at the intersection of many other, interconnected crises. Chief among these is the global climate crisis, which evidence suggests will have complex and unpredictable impacts on cooperation and conflict across the world, while putting pressure on sustainable food systems. Wider humanitarian crises, too, that we might think of chiefly as displacement or health crises, often entail the targeting of food systems. In 2018, for example, the UN's Assistant Secretary-General for Human Rights concluded that tactics of "forced starvation" had been employed in the violent campaign against the Rohingya people in Myanmar, leading more than 800,000 to seek refuge in neighbouring Bangladesh. Lastly, conflict-driven food crises are linked to a subject I want to discuss in greater detail today: the gendered nature of war and humanitarian emergency.

Overview

Today, both global conflict and acute hunger are increasing. By almost any metric, the world is more insecure in 2020 than it was a decade ago. Violent conflict is becoming both more prevalent, and more complex. Today's conflicts are often of lower intensity in terms of casualties, but are highly fragmented, multi-actor, and often protracted crises.

These crises are driving an increase in acute hunger. In recent years, after decades of improvement in levels of world hunger, we are seeing a sustained increase in hunger globally. In an era some believed might have heralded the end of famine, not only are we not making progress on the Sustainable Development Goal of zero hunger but, as Deputy Secretary General Amina Mohammed noted recently, we are going in reverse.

And make no mistake, violent conflict is the cause. Conflict is the largest single driver of severe food insecurity worldwide and the main driver for over two-thirds of people in food crises. By the most recent count, there are 74 million acutely food-insecure people in 21 conflict-affected countries.

Beyond being the primary driver globally, violent conflict is the defining characteristic of the world's worst food crises. In Yemen, for example, the World Food Programme has launched its largest-ever emergency response. On average, the proportion of under-nourished people is almost three times as high in countries in conflict and protracted crisis than in other low-income contexts. Countries in Africa, where historically, much of Ireland's development cooperation has been focused, remain disproportionately affected by food crises.

In other words, it is not just that conflict is hunger's most significant driver and is therefore central to the ambition of getting to zero hunger. But, reaching the furthest behind first depends on addressing hunger in conflict-affected contexts, where these crises are worst and where people are most vulnerable.

In 2017, the UN warned of the imminent risk of famine in four countries (South Sudan, Somalia, north-east Nigeria and Yemen), all devastated by violent conflict. The announcement resulted in UN Member States mobilising to draft, and ultimately unanimously pass, UN Security Council Resolution 2417 on the protection of civilians placing a central focus on the prohibition of food as a weapon of war. UNSCR 2417 is a clear indication that the international community is outraged by the tragedy of preventable famine in the twenty-first century and galvanised into effective action when the prospect of food crisis at this scale arises. The coordinated action and momentum in responding was extraordinary. On the ground, humanitarian teams worked tirelessly to scale-up efforts, save lives and draw attention to deteriorating conditions.

Since that time, further progress has been made on the World Bank's Famine Action Mechanism seeking to tie early warning of future food crises to the timely dispersal of funds. At the International Criminal Court, the Assembly of States Parties endorsed an amendment to the Rome Statute recognising, for the first time, starvation as a war crime in non-international armed conflicts. However, it should not require the spectre of four famines to mobilise global action. Nor should this scale of suffering be required to ensure vital momentum is maintained in the aftermath.

Pathways

Before I speak about the way forward and future action, I want to dedicate some time to discussing the pathways through which conflict produces hunger. This is important for three reasons.

First, from the perspective of a social scientist, I want to be accurate in diagnosing the challenge we face. Without understanding the precise mechanisms through which conflict causes hunger, we cannot hope to fully understand them. Second, from the perspective of a humanitarian, I want to expedite effective response. Without identifying clear mechanisms, we cannot meaningfully address root causes, target prevention and support recovery. And third, from the perspective of an advocate to policymakers, I want to be clear that there is nothing natural or inevitable about conflict causing hunger. Conflict does not automatically lead to food crises: they can and must be prevented and made both morally—and politically—unacceptable.

The first pathway—often the most extreme and visible—is the use of food as a strategic weapon of war. This includes the deliberate targeting of food supplies, agricultural land and livestock, and food storage infrastructure by parties to a conflict. It can also include preventing or restricting the movement of food supplies, and wilfully impeding humanitarian relief. The work of groups like Global Rights Compliance and the World Peace Foundation in documenting instances of this point to the use of this tactic in high-intensity, large-scale and often regionalised conflicts, such as in Yemen, South Sudan and Syria.

The second pathway—which is not entirely independent from the first—is through smaller-scale, often localised conflicts. We know that conflicts are becoming more diffuse and characterised by greater fragmentation. A more diverse constellation of state and non-state actors pose a greater risk to civilians and create a more challenging environment for humanitarian negotiation, coordination and access. Conflicts between livelihood groups, centring on natural resources or livestock, can fall into this category, as can relatively low-intensity violence that disrupts food and market systems. Critically, we know that national crises and local-level conflict systems often intersect and fuel each other, with sometimes devastating effects. Even where large-scale conflict is driven by wider, geopolitical factors, food and food systems can become flashpoints of violence in local livelihood systems. This means that this pathway is widespread across insecure and fragile contexts.

The third—and often the least visible—pathway is through social mechanisms. Here, I am indebted to Ireland's Department of Foreign Affairs and Trade's development cooperation funding, which supported research conducted as part of Concern Worldwide's work in South Sudan. That work highlighted the ways in which conflict causes hunger far from the frontlines of fighting, and often in hidden ways. This research revealed ways that social solidarity mechanisms are transformed and disrupted by conflict. Where once, loans of food, sharing of available supplies, or mutual support in times of stress might have buoyed vulnerable households, collective support systems—between community members, neighbours, and even family—can collapse in conflict. This can occur through a breakdown of trust, the upheaval of displacement, and pressure on limited resources.

This has particular implications for those already at the margins of social networks even before crises set in, such as the elderly, or people living with disabilities or conditions that are stigmatised. As before, this is a reminder of the sharp meeting points between the reality of conflict and hunger, and our ambition of reaching the furthest behind first. This also has starkly gendered dimensions, including through the unequal distribution of food within the household—with men and boys receiving more, better or earlier food than women and girls; an increased risk of intimate partner violence and violence in the household in a context of wider social strain; and gendered violence through distress coping strategies like child marriage. In many rural contexts, women also carry greater responsibility for household food security and manual agricultural labour, while at the same time, enjoying disproportionately fewer land rights than men.

These mechanisms are no less important to the discussion of conflict and hunger for being less direct, and sometimes less visible. They are also a vital reminder of the different entry points available to the international community in seeking to address this crisis.

The Way Forward

In 2008, in the wake of the global food price crisis, Ireland's Hunger Task Force produced a report aimed at identifying the specific contribution Ireland could make to tackling the root causes of hunger, particularly in Africa. A decade later, the world faces another food crisis, this time driven by violent conflict. Today, what does an ambitious agenda to address conflict-driven hunger look like?

Against the backdrop of a mounting crisis, it is important that Ireland recognise its own experience of conflict and hunger and become a powerful advocate for crisis-affected communities on the global stage. In two short years, Ireland will commemorate the 175th anniversary of the Great Famine. An tUachtarán Higgins spoke in this very lecture series of how "*this memory of our past has shaped and has continued to shape our values and our sensibilities today, instilling in us a moral calling to help others in need.*"

In its report, the Hunger Task Force identified a failure of governance at national and international levels for ongoing global hunger, specifically citing an apparent willingness to live with the current extent of global hunger. Ten years later, little has changed globally in this regard, and reversing this, first requires a shift in thinking. Member states, and the international community as a whole, must recognise severe food crises as the pressing security issue that they are. Hunger is not incidental to contemporary violent conflict: it is a tactic employed by warring parties, a product of localised conflict systems, and a deep-rooted consequence of conflict's social impacts.

In responding, Ireland and other member states should focus action in three key areas:

• Supporting humanitarian response tailored to conflict contexts;

• Strengthening reporting and accountability at the UN Security Council and beyond; and

• Leveraging policy synergies of existing agendas, particularly in relation to the gendered dimensions of conflict and hunger.

Tailored humanitarian programming

As a donor, and a key partner to communities in the midst of, and emerging from, violent conflict, Ireland can support principled humanitarian response to food crises in several ways.

First, there is a clear need for greater investment in conflict-sensitive livelihood and food security responses. Livelihood and food security programming must be tailored to the conflict context in order to reduce pressure on natural resources and food systems, build and reinforce often depleted social capital, and support the capacity of crisis-affected communities to better anticipate, adapt to, and recover from conflict shocks and their impacts on their food security.

Conflict analysis needs to be undertaken, fully resourced and regularly updated and monitored as a central part of humanitarian response. We cannot work in conflict, and ensure we are having a positive impact, if we do not understand conflict dynamics. But too often, humanitarian systems are overstretched and actors lack the space, time, and resources needed for in-depth analysis and critical reflection. We should not consider conflict analysis as outside the core functions of humanitarian organisations: it must inform humanitarian response so we know which livelihood systems make people more or less vulnerable to attack, which assets can generate more or less competition in communities, and which systems of participation selection and vulnerability analysis have greater or lesser legitimacy.

This is important at every level: during conflict, even far from armed fighting, the potential for localised tensions to result in significant humanitarian suffering should not be underestimated. And long after war is officially over, violence continues for many in their communities, families, and homes. Considering that most people in conflict-affected countries depend on agriculture for their livelihoods, it is particularly important that transitions out of conflict take better account of sustainable and conflict-sensitive livelihood strategies for the reintegration of former combatants, their families and communities, and displacement-affected populations. Livelihood resilience programmes especially adapted to conflict contexts—to anticipate, adapt, and recover from conflict—are a vital part of this transition. We know that national peacebuilding processes cannot consolidate peace unless there is local buy-in and ground-up participation and leadership. Without responses tailored to local peace and conflict dynamics, we may continue to see localised devastation of livelihoods and nutrition outcomes even where national-level peace is established.

More evidence and learning in this area would be valuable; and key global platforms and fora, such as discussions surrounding the FAO

Framework for Action for Food Security and Nutrition in Protracted Crises, Tokyo's Nutrition for Growth Summit in 2020, and New York's Food Systems Summit in 2021, can all provide opportunities to share expertise and deepen global action in this area.

Existing legal instruments, reporting, and accountability

At a global policy level, we have no shortage of laws and policy instruments in which the right to food is enshrined. This right is recognised in international humanitarian law, which explicitly prohibits the starvation of civilians as a weapon of war, including the wilful impediment of relief supplies. It is also codified in multiple provisions of international human rights law, including the Convention on the Rights of the Child, and the International Covenant on Economic, Social and Cultural Rights.

Individual UN Resolutions—both global in scope, such as UNSCR 2417, and country-focused, such as resolutions on Syria, Yemen, Somalia, South Sudan, and DRC—have also served as important mechanisms for drawing attention to the scale of conflict-driven food crises and mandating action.

We do not lack provisions and instruments of international law. What we lack is robust monitoring, effective reporting, and political commitment to conflict prevention and resolution. Member states can make better use of existing monitoring and reporting systems to draw attention to the importance of food in these fora and mechanisms. For example, member states can draw attention to the right to food through the Human Rights Council's Universal Period Review; and through country-specific and thematic reviews by the Peacebuilding Commission. Leveraging these existing mechanisms is vital to reinforcing the norm that conflict-driven food crises are not inevitable or natural, but avoidable and unacceptable.

Existing frameworks, and the Women, Peace and Security Agenda

Related to this, I want to draw your attention to a particular opportunity for the international community to make progress on addressing conflict-driven food crises: the Women, Peace and Security

(WPS) agenda. This year, we are marking the twentieth anniversary of UNSCR 1325. We know that there is still a long way to go before we can claim to have arrived at a full understanding of the gendered nature and impacts of insecurity, the most effective actions to prevent and reduce gendered violence in conflict in all its forms, and the transformative potential of women's leadership in conflict resolution and peacebuilding. But, of those issues that have generated political momentum and begun to translate into global, national, and local action, UNSCR 1325 and associated resolutions have had extraordinary success.

And effective advocates find strong allies. I want each of you to ask yourselves, where is hunger in the WPS agenda? I propose that meaningful progress in addressing conflict and hunger can come through a greater attention to WPS in two ways:

Frist, as I have outlined above, and many studies have documented, both conflict and hunger are profoundly gendered. It is vital that in considering the gendered drivers of conflict, the gendered impacts of humanitarian crises, and the potential for gender-transformative peace, that we consider access to, control over, and utilisation of food. For example, humanitarian and development programmes aimed at advancing gender equality can do more to engage with food security and livelihood obstacles that differentially affect women, men, girls, and boys.

Further, reporting at national and global levels on initiatives, frameworks, and action plans to protect, support, and empower women in conflict can consider in more detail how women's right to food has been affected by insecurity, and where conflict's legacy produces and maintains gendered gaps in the full enjoyment of this right. Ireland's Third National Action Plan on Women, Peace and Security explicitly recognises that,

Conflict and hunger are inextricably linked. Food can also be used as a weapon of war. Women and girls are frequently responsible for agricultural production and feeding families and are particularly vulnerable to food insecurity.

But it is in the minority. In a review of a database of National Action Plans on Women, Peace and Security compiled by Caitlin Hamilton, Nyibeny Naam and Laura J. Shepherd, of the 59 NAPs published in the last five years, just over one-third specifically mentioned food, hunger, or starvation. That means that in the five-year period since the world made getting to zero hunger, and achieving gender equality, global goals, only one-in-three NAPs have explicitly recognised the link between these two. Even among those that do, the majority mention food only in passing. Far fewer reference hunger, fewer still mention starvation, even though we know this is a long-established, profoundly gendered, and devastating tactic in contemporary warfare.

Second, as I have mentioned, the WPS agenda has been remarkably successful in mobilising action and focusing political attention. So even beyond the specific gendered dimensions of food security in conflict, we can learn from the lessons of WPS for any global initiative. It seems to me that there are several key lessons to highlight that have important parallels in how we address conflict and hunger.

The first is that while UNSCR 1325 was a watershed moment, it was not an isolated one. It took incremental change over decades to build up a body of resolutions and global policy that meant real progress on this issue was launched and sustained. This should serve as an important caution that if we want UNSCR 2417 to be impactful, we must look ahead to the complementary and targeted instruments required to consolidate and strengthen it in the years to come. And we must identify the member state champions who will show the political leadership and initiative to safeguard this progress.

The second lesson is that although the WPS agenda is localised through National Action Plans, we still too often see a disconnect between global rhetoric and national action. For too many women in crisis, the aims of UNSCR 1325 remain too remote to make a meaningful difference in their lives, and their voices have been too marginal in high-level discussions. This should be a lesson to us all that crisis-affected communities must be at the centre of any policy or response. We must avoid the trap of thinking of populations whose right to food has been violated merely as passive recipients of global policy, and as too vulnerable to claim ownership and lead in its development. Real progress will rest on centering crisis-affected communities and supporting complementary food and conflict resolution systems that are best-suited to their needs, aspirations and recovery.

The third lesson is that we must expand our understanding of the dimensions of violent conflict. Although abhorrent, a narrow focus on the most direct elements of gendered violence can serve to obscure the many complex social systems that prevent true gender equality and wider social transformation. We must recognise that even in conflict, for example, women are often more vulnerable to violence in their own homes than outside of them. Similar patterns are becoming clear in relation to food crises: the targeted use of food as a weapon of war is legally prohibited, morally unacceptable, and devastating in impact. Beyond this, the complex ways that local conflict systems and social power relations in crisis interact with food availability, access, utilisation, and stability are too often overlooked and yet continue to undermine food security and recovery for millions of people.

Lastly, the success of the WPS agenda can point us to responses that should be explored in relation to conflict and hunger. This will be valuable in building a more central gendered perspective into our response to food crises, introducing the question of hunger and food security more prominently in the WPS agenda, and better leveraging synergies between the two.

At a global level, member states should consider specialised training for peacekeeping troops on conflict-driven food crises, and the deployment of specialist hunger technical staff in missions, mirroring the vital investment in gender capacity across UN forces. The creation of a Special Advisor to the UN Secretary-General on conflict and food crises would complement the vital work of the outgoing Special Rapporteur on the Right to Food, and help to draw attention to the issue globally. The open, annual debate on Women, Peace and Security at the UN has been vital in setting a global agenda, and may have parallels in high-level discussions on food security that could provide a focal point for diverse action and advocacy efforts in this area.

In supporting peace processes bilaterally and multilaterally, member states should place greater emphasis on food security, hunger, and starvation, which remain relatively neglected. WPS advocates have monitored the inclusion and leadership of women in peace processes, in part by drawing attention to their exclusion in delegations, and the silence of official peace agreements on gendered provisions of disarmament, reconciliation, reintegration, and recovery. That silence is also found in relation to food security: in a database of over 1,800 peace agreements compiled by Christine Bell and others at the University of Edinburgh, the term 'food' appears in the texts of only 160 agreements (fewer than 10% of all agreements coded). 'Hunger' appears in the texts of only 11 agreements, 'famine' in only seven, and 'starvation' in only two. Many of these records concern multiple agreements in the same conflict, meaning the actual number of member states that have explicitly recognised the right to food or freedom from hunger, and mechanisms to prevent and recover from famine or starvation in peace processes, is even fewer still.

Ultimately, much more must be done to bring together advocates of women's protection and equality, and those focused on bringing an end to conflict-driven food crises, whose goals are so clearly aligned. While formal, written inclusion in policies and frameworks such as resolutions, peace agreements, and National Action Plans alone is insufficient to ensure meaningful change, it is almost impossible without it.

Conclusion

It may occur to you in reflecting on what I've shared, that Ireland is already leading in many areas critical to progress on conflict-driven food crises. Our role in the SDG development and commitment to reach the furthest behind first means that we have an obligation to not only address hunger, but focus our efforts in responding to the greatest and gravest food crises—those driven by conflict.

Our technical leadership in global nutrition and hunger policy, coupled with our own experience of conflict and famine, lend us an authentic voice and national experience in this area, at a time when there is all too often a retreat from global multilateralism and a perceived disconnect between domestic policy and international development cooperation.

Lastly, our leadership in the Women, Peace and Security agenda demands that we ask—what are the gendered dimensions of conflict and hunger? And beyond that, as a leading voice at the UN on this topic, what are the lessons from the significant progress in the field of Women, Peace and Security that might help us forge the path to zero hunger?

Go raibh maith agaibh.

—Dublin, March 2020

The Conflict of Hunger

Matthew Hollingworth
Representative & Country Director, South Sudan
World Food Programme

Anne-Laure Duval
Global Head of Protection
World Food Programme

(This paper reflects the views of the authors and not that of the World Food Programme)

This paper brings a practitioner's perspective on the relationship between hunger and conflict. What follows are reflections and a few suggestions drawn from close to twenty years of field experience, serving the World Food Programme as the representative in Syria, Sudan and currently South Sudan.

We seek to highlight some of the challenges humanitarian practitioners face in addressing hunger in the context of conflict and suggest how we might improve the international community's approach. Three potential avenues for action are identified:

- First, to consider how the international community might better harness collective knowledge and analysis to inform a more effective response;
- Second, to reflect how donors might reframe how their humanitarian and development assistance is premised and delivered; and
- Third, to consider how jurisprudence can give content to the political commitment of Security Council Resolution 2417 and the subsequent amendment of Article 8 of the Rome Statute, elevating starvation from a weapon of war to a war crime, including in situations of non-international armed conflict.

Hunger and Conflict

The Narrative

The international community is accustomed to thinking of hunger as a side effect of conflict. However, side effects are effects. The use of "side" distracts from the reality. In simple numerical terms, hunger is often more deadly than that inflicted by weapons, yet the drama and clamor of war obscure the quieter tragedy of famine and starvation. Wars and explicit violence capture the headlines, and our attention, in a way that hunger sometimes fails to do. Some examples, which are both familiar and yet unfamiliar: more Vietnamese died in the Tonkin famine of 1943-44 than in the terrible—yet far better known—conflicts that followed. During World War II, in Europe, Asia, and Africa, conflict-related deaths—just shy of 20 million—were equaled, and perhaps eclipsed, by a similar toll from hunger. Alarming figures can also be found for contemporary or ongoing conflicts in Sudan, South Sudan, Somalia, Nigeria and Yemen. These figures are startling, because for reasons that are unfathomable, deaths from famine are less visible, less newsworthy—less memorable than death by gun, bomb, or shell. The point, simply, is that war's impact on food security is as deadly as war itself.

Reference is made to World War II because this is in our living memory and it brought together the international community to address its failures. It was in the wake of World War II that the United Nations was established. The international community wanted to ensure that the atrocities of that magnitude never happen again. Despite many shortcomings and failures, the UN system has alleviated the toll of some appalling crises and conflicts. The international humanitarian community evolved, and today is structured and funded on the premise of treating hunger largely as a side effect of conflict. Conflict creates the need; humanitarians respond accordingly.

In this context, the World Food Programme was established within the multilateral system as the food delivery operational arm of the United Nations Food and Agriculture Organisation (FAO). It has always been perceived as the logistical engine that feeds the hungry.

Yet, from the outset of its creation, despite initially being an experimental three-year programme, WFP was mandated with first, saving lives; second, improving the nutrition and quality of life of the most vulnerable people at critical times in their lives; and third, helping build self-reliance of poor people and communities. WFP now describes its role as "saving lives, changing lives." Nevertheless, already in the 1960s, it was acknowledged that peoples' needs can vary, and thus, WFP assistance should adapt to those needs.

Increases in food prices do not affect all people equally. Thus, those most negatively affected by a food crisis are the poorest of the poor, as they are least able to purchase higher-priced food. When no other poverty indicators are available, WFP considers that the world's most vulnerable, who spend 60 percent of their income on food, are inevitably priced out of the food market. To be able to assist these people adequately, WFP needs to understand why these people are poor and not limit the analysis to expenditure on a food basket. Yet, the instruments and the definition of people in need have largely been grounded in calorific adequacy. To change lives meaningfully, a deeper understanding of social dynamics and power struggles is required.

The architecture of the humanitarian system is built on the premise of identifying need and responding accordingly. Our understanding of hunger must evolve and become multi-dimensional. In the case of conflict and hunger, this is more apparent. It has become inescapable that the relationship between hunger and conflict is far more complex and dynamic than the binary cause-and-effect schema outlined above. This complexity has not yet been adequately reflected in the humanitarian architecture, nor in the nature of the needs WFP is mandated to address.

Hunger is a direct result of conflict. Conversely, food security is a prerequisite for a state's socio-economic security, and as such, food insecurity can intensify and, at times, cause conflict. The corollary for humanitarian actors, donors and practitioners, is that treating hunger simply as a side effect of conflict is inadequate, and ill-suited, to both the scale and the nature of the problem. It is therefore time for us, the international community, as academics, donors, and practitioners, to adapt our thinking, and our response, accordingly.

The Legal and Policy Framework

Hunger comes when the four elements of food security have disappeared—availability, stability, access and utilization, as defined in the 1996 World Food Summit. Or within a rights framework, when the five elements of the right to food are missing, namely: availability, stability, accessibility, sustainability and adequacy—acknowledged in WFP's 2012 Protection Policy and in the Inter-Agency Standing Committee's (IASC) Centrality of Protection Strategy. Inequalities, with disparities in income and wealth and access to basic needs, such as food, shelter and clothing, but also sanitation, education, healthcare, and justice are growing. The achievement of real, visible and long-lasting development is severely constrained. To understand the drivers of these inequalities, WFP strives to ensure that people of concern are central to all decisions and delivery related to its food security mandate, whether in humanitarian, development or protracted crisis settings.

The legal framework at the international community's disposal gives the multilateral system the scope to examine the complexities of food insecurity in conflict. Some of the core components of hunger fall beyond WFP's remit or mandate—the organisational DNA—but as the largest operational food security agency mainly responding in conflict and protracted settings, WFP must consider all aspects of hunger, mainly, why people are hungry.

By way of illustration: in Syria, it is now well established that the collapse of food systems was an underestimated and poorly understood element of both the long and short-term unfolding of socio-political and humanitarian crises. Before the war broke out, over the period of 2010-2012, droughts had occurred across Syria displacing the rural poor to the urban areas. This rapid urbanization of people who were losing their livelihoods exposed the disparities in wealth and social inequalities which should have served as an early warning for a potential conflict. When analysis of the unfolding situation eventually did occur, food security was a missing link. More specifically, food security was not factored as a key element driving displacement, urbanization, refugee outflow, economic and or social collapse. Yet, WFP in Syria was responding to people's immediate need to be fed; it was not WFP's role to question whether the lack of food or collapse of food systems was one of the origins of the tensions.

The Analysis

The case of Syria, and this understanding of the dynamic, interdependent relationship of hunger and conflict, has significant implications, not only for our understanding of the genesis of conflict, but also for the ways humanitarians and practitioners should respond.

A metaphor helps to illustrate. Like focusing only on the second and third acts of a three-act play, most conflict research focuses on conflict dynamics already evolving in an ongoing conflict. Studying the first act—meaning understanding the setting, acquiring an understanding of who the actors are, what their everyday life is like, and what is important to them—rarely happens. Typically, the international aid community does not answer these questions. It skips that step and rushes into a response on the basis of urgent, existing and identifiable needs. Answering some of these questions through collective research would provide practical insights into Act II, which is typically the Confrontation, Rising Action, and Act III, the Resolution. Extending the metaphor, a focus on Act I could help inform responses and possibly help reduce the scale of conflict, through harnessing collective knowledge and using it to design creative "out-of-the box" projects and programmes. Identifying the reasons for inequality is a first step but then, we as a community should not just state them, but use them to design more creative ways of responding.

Deeper research and analysis would bring to light the fact that hunger is one of the factors that leads to civil unrest or conflict. While not the only factor, it is a key constituent in socio-political stability. This has been unmistakable in the last decade, in 2008, when food prices spiked, followed by a surge in civil unrest across a swathe of lower and middle-income countries. "Angry consumers took to the streets in at least 48 nations across Africa, Asia and the Caribbean." Finally, some contend that the Arab Spring was linked to an increase in food prices. When people took to the streets in Egypt in 2011, they shouted: عيش حرية عدالة اجتماعية "Bread, Freedom and Social Justice."

The existing tools that the humanitarian community uses to determine humanitarian needs do not support analysis to inform decision-making. The resources given by the donor community and the measurement of the success of allocations are linked to quantities of food or medicines delivered and to the number of people who have received them over a short time period. Time to understand what has happened is not afforded to the humanitarian on the ground, and most of the time, it is not seen as his or her job. Additional expertise and data have not been brought to bear to examine and respond appropriately; accordingly, there is a need for suitably interdisciplinary, inter-agency research to help join the dots followed by new programmatic models and designs. Accurate treatment follows from accurate diagnosis, and so too the reverse: in Syria, both the international response and programmes have been accordingly mismatched and ill-equipped to meet the nature of the challenge of Syria's breakdown and collapse.

The Practice

Drawing from these and other examples from the field, we offer a few suggestions as to how WFP might tailor a more effective and appropriate response. The use of hunger as a weapon of war is probably as old as war itself. Examples abound today, such as besiegement of key logistics hubs (like ports) and communities themselves—cutting people off from access to food and markets. The shattering of livelihoods through scorched-earth tactics, inhibiting communities' ability to cope and frequently causing destitution and displacement, is commonplace. The tactic of starving people is brutal and yet horribly effective, causing lasting and devastating impact. A week of war—or even just the perceived risk of danger—during the planting or harvesting season can bring a year or longer of hunger to a community.

Such tactics frequently pass unnoticed due to the swiftness of their execution. This type of tactic is cheaper, but just as viciously effective as fighting a war with bombs and bullets.

To induce hunger in large civilian populations in sieges was a common tactic in Syria. The siege and starvation of Madaya received extensive media coverage. In February 2020, the assault on Idlib has featured restrictions on food assistance, burning crops and farmable land described as literally "burning all aspects of life." Through the course of the Syrian conflict many other locations have been subjected to the same destructive tactics. The main purpose is to exert pressure on an opposition group to force them to surrender, for example, by besieging locations. The parties to the conflict are dissimulated among civilians who are "just" civilian casualties. In Syria's Eastern Ghouta, the Government cut off water supplies, targeted communal kitchens and bakeries, and either restricted or even blocked food assistance. All these measures had had the sole purpose of inflicting incremental, and often, eventually complete deprivation.

In South Sudan, by the end of 2015, nearly 1.5 million people and a further 730,000 had been forcibly displaced or fled across South Sudan's borders. Approximately ten percent of those seeking protection sought refuge in UN Protection of Civilians sites, with much larger numbers displacing. In Unity State, "many hid in the swamps and cases of drowning were reported as people sought to collect water lilies for food or to hide from soldiers." Although there was disagreement over how such deaths should be recorded, it was decided that they could not be attributed to famine, as neither hunger nor hunger-related illness was their direct cause.

In Syria, WFP's approach was to "stay and deliver"—an approach which was criticized, as it was seen as only serving people in government-controlled areas where it had physical access. WFP was thus perceived as siding with one of the parties to the conflict. From the inside, the reality was much different. For one, the people, mainly civilians residing in government-held areas, were not necessarily affiliated with the government. From the outside, the humanitarian community was not seen as neutral. Nuances of what responders were dealing with were, however, not understood or perhaps poorly documented and communicated. In a theatre of operation, deliberate and conscious trade-offs are made. Syria, prior to the war, was well on its way to meet the Millennium Development Goals (MDGs). The need for humanitarian non-governmental organisations (NGOs) was not existent, which means that aside from the Red Crescent, there were close to no partners on the ground who could effectively deliver humanitarian assistance. That was the reason WFP decided to "stay and deliver." As a protection-mandated agency, it was also trying to support the delivery of medical supplies. The World Health Organisation (WHO) was allowed to distribute medicine, but was prevented from delivering much-needed surgical materials which the authorities considered would be used for supporting combatants and thus politically motivated. There is no perfect answer, but these are the issues and tensions that a representative on the ground has to deal with and balance to make the best decision possible without always receiving the required support from Headquarters, often due to a misreading or lack of understanding of the nuances on the ground.

In another example, Sudan, in the months that led to the overthrow of President Bashir, the first riots in the streets of Khartoum were triggered by the lifting of the wheat subsidy, which resulted in a stark increase in the price of bread. People tend to assume that the poor, the hungry and the most vulnerable will riot. In the case of Sudan, the middle class commonly consumes bread and lives in urban settings where it is easier to congregate. The poor live off sorghum. The riots took place in urban Khartoum or Nyala (the second largest city in Sudan), where the standard of living is higher than in the rest of the country. This shows that unrest and riots can be linked sometimes mainly to what people feel entitled to rather than to a loss of material security. Earlier on in Sudan's history in Darfur, Khartoum did not anticipate the uprising of Darfurians, contending that they were "too hungry to stage an armed revolution." The traders (the Zaghawa) across the Chad-Darfur border had built a considerable amount of wealth which had gone unnoticed by the Government in Khartoum.

There is no mechanistic or inevitable relationship between conflict and hunger. Spikes in food prices frequently, but not inevitably, lead to unrest. The immediate response of a government can be to draw from its National Grain Reserve or call on WFP to strengthen its food assistance programme. This approach is only a redistribution and does nothing to solve the underlying issue of supply and eventual equitable distribution. In the case of Sudan, the government turned to its neighbour the Kingdom of Saudia Arabia to provide financial support—again a temporary fix. Worse, these temporary solutions can sometimes detract from addressing the root causes of the problem. They were, as the media terminology puts it, "band-aids," not solutions. In Sudan, WFP's approach at the time was to try and address both the immediate needs of those who were hungry and advocate for heightened attention to the country, which is a forgotten crisis in comparison with Syria, Yemen or South Sudan. In Sudan, the international community's role was to advocate for international support. Concessional finance was unavailable from the International Monetary Fund and the World Bank, as Sudan was in arrears on account of bearing the debt of South Sudan. Sudan's continued presence on the United States State Sponsors of Terrorism list made it difficult to achieve debt relief and restart International Financial Institution grants and loans. Many traditional donors limited their assistance to humanitarian support, while others used partners to deliver aid outside of government systems. Consequently, there were few incentives, or conditions, to encourage or help the government to engage in sufficient macro-economic reform.

The United Nations Country Team in Sudan with donors had offered an *interim* arrangement to support the economy and prevent more people from falling into poverty as well as potential civil war. While economic reforms were, and remain, necessary irrespective of the availability of external financing, the United Nations, World Bank, European Union, the United States Agency for International Development (USAID), and the United Kingdom Department for International Development (DFID) in Khartoum worked on a proposal for a facility to help Sudan deliver a managed programme of reforms and address their social and economic impact. This facility would have been governed by an agreement between the international community and the Government of Sudan. The proposal asserted a number of pre-conditions that stipulated the necessary macro-economic reforms and the political reforms agreed between the international community and the Government of Sudan accompanied by continued and re-focused support from traditional partners with increased humanitarian assistance and social safety nets to provide immediate respite to the poorest during the reform period. This initiative never materialised despite being creative and forward thinking. The lack of willingness to expose difficult choices, the need to be creative, coupled with the effort and energy to achieve results, can often slow down a practitioner in the field. A country representative will no doubt suffer from advocacy fatigue, meaning that despite efforts to deliberately weigh decisions and consider the best options, practitioners inside a theatre of operations are possibly heard but not listened to.

Leveraging the Humanitarian-Development-Peace Nexus

The first part of this paper has considered some of the complexities practitioners face at the field level. These challenges range from understanding a context to being equipped by the international community with the necessary financing and measurement tools to address the problems even when they have been identified and understood.

This section of the paper examines the humanitarian-development-peace nexus and how it can be leveraged to respond effectively to some of these complexities. "The nexus focuses on the work needed to coherently address people's vulnerability before, during and after crises." It is supposed to provide the link between development projects and humanitarian activities. To date, humanitarian funds typically have been stretched to cover development projects, particularly in protracted crises, inadequately assisting the people in the most vulnerable situations.

Both WFP's mandate and the definition of the right to food support the development of a richer and more effective understanding of the relationship between conflict and food. The Paris Declaration on aid effectiveness and the Accra Agenda for Action, followed and reinforced by the Busan partnership for effective development cooperation require that donor countries ensure that their investments are focused on results—that they have a lasting impact on eradicating poverty and reducing inequality, on sustainable development, and on enhancing developing countries' capacities, aligned with the priorities and policies set out by developing countries themselves. These agreements also call for inclusive development partnerships and the recognition of the different and complementary roles of all actors. The content of these declarations and action plans show that the international community understands the multi-faceted issues a practitioner deals with and their localisation or contextualisation.

Yet, bridging the humanitarian-development-peace nexus remains an elusive goal due to the current aid architecture, because, without achieving a transition from humanitarian action to development, including peace building assistance, fragile situations do not improve. It is time for the international community to adapt to maintain its relevance. The International Network on Conflict and Fragility (INCAF) created nearly ten years ago is a good example of attempting to bring about change. One of INCAF's welcome efforts has been to work hand-in-hand with partners through the g7+ and in the International Dialogue. Political leadership and advocacy through INCAF and the g7+ helped ensure that conflict and fragility concerns were integrated into the SDGs, as manifested in Goal 16. WFP has recognised that it can contribute to this discussion by bringing to the table ways to integrate operational reality into policy. In this way, WFP can support donors to change behaviour, particularly in having a coherent approach to humanitarian-development-peace and security outcomes.

The 2030 Agenda, grounded in the principle of leaving no one behind, and the Grand Bargain Commitments are further manifestations of the international community's understanding of the fact that issues cannot be dealt with in isolation. The nexus merely reaffirms what has been known for years, that there is a continuum—international assistance is dynamic. The purpose of these commitments is mainly to confine humanitarian funding to finance humanitarian action. As illustrated by the Sudan example, development is an area that practitioners—particularly in conflict settings—tend to shy away from, for the simple reason that development must be aligned to national priorities and initiatives. Often development actors are working with a government that is a party to a conflict, which in a nexus setting, will compromise the humanitarian principle of neutrality.

These challenges are serious, but not—certainly not always—insurmountable. There is momentum thanks to the humanitarian-development-peace nexus, but the thinking behind the nexus has not sufficiently matured. The triple nexus is a way to recall the three pillars the UN is built on: human rights, peace and security, and development. Attention and investment should be given to each component, yet today, only three percent of the UN's budget is devoted to human rights. Similarly, investment is made in humanitarian assistance, which by nature is punctual and supposed to be short-term. Different mechanisms should be designed to support longer-term objectives. If flexible financing mechanisms were in place with realistic time frames to show progress built in, some of the difficulties laid out above could be overcome.

With adequate resourcing and time, WFP could conduct more comprehensive analysis on food insecurity, detailing the threats faced by populations to physical, material and legal safety beyond vulnerability to food insecurity. Robust context analysis that is regularly updated will enable protection and people-centred responses to evolve as situations change. As a result, through its programmes, WFP could contribute to reduce, and where possible, prevent people's vulnerability to food insecurity, inequality and exclusion. This approach would also allow WFP to integrate mechanisms that ensure the long-term sustainability of its programming. Such analysis would also determine when WFP's role should be advocacy, rather than direct operational engagement—i.e. when WFP should and can leverage its size and scope to support and partner with other actors that have other specializations to ensure a coordinated and complementary approach.

Opportunities for Accountability

May 2020 will mark the two-year anniversary of the adoption of Security Council Resolution 2417. This protective resolution was the result of years of lobbying, coupled with the concern about the increase in duration and number of conflicts. It offers the practitioners on the ground an opportunity to hold the international community accountable for taking action, when deprivation of access to food is occurring. Under the umbrella of the protection of civilians, according to the guidance on the resolution, the Secretary General must report to the Security Council on the risk of famine and food insecurity in countries with armed conflict, as part of his regular reporting on country specific situations.

The guidance on the implementation of the resolution requires reporting on incidences of destruction of objects necessary for life—food production, processing or distribution, as well as incidences of humanitarian agencies being denied access to populations that are in need of life-saving assistance by warring parties, either directly (*e.g.* roadblocks) or indirectly (*e.g.* through bureaucratic impediments). This new obligation to report requires WFP to understand food insecurity in a broad sense and to be able to determine from patterns and trends when there is an intent to deprive populations from access to food. The reporting guidance provides an avenue that did not exist at the start of the Syrian war to support the protection-mandate agencies such as WFP to take a decision to stay and deliver.

Currently, WFP is using the Integrated Food Security Phase Classification (IPC) as the tool to determine levels of food insecurity. It examines three different scales: acute food insecurity, which threatens lives or livelihoods; chronic food insecurity, which focuses on quality and quantity of food consumption for an active and healthy life; and acute malnutrition. The IPC was developed to provide an understanding of the severity of food security against which funding would be sought. The IPC has five phases:

Phase One: Normal; Phase Two: Stressed; Phase Three: Crisis; Phase Four: Emergency; and Phase Five: Famine. To reach the stage of Famine within the IPC, at least twenty percent of the population have no access to food; at least thirty percent of children under five years are moderately or severely wasted; and two or more people/10,000 are dying per day due to famine related causes. Or more colloquially put, famine is distinct from the other phases by conditions of destitution—a collapse in coping mechanisms and a large increase in mortality. As such, famine, or Phase Five, is equated with starvation, when in fact, people may die of hunger or related causes in other phases, particularly phases Three and Four. This means "starvation" related deaths are not clear.

A recent analysis of the IPC explains that while the IPC is a good tool, it is restrictive, because it focuses mainly on severity and is heavily quantitative. In South Sudan, when famine was declared in February 2017 in two counties, and subsequently declared ended in those counties three months later, the IPC Phase Three had risen from 4 million to 5.5 million people across the country. This shows that severity is important, but duration, magnitude and geographic locations are also qualitative dimensions that need to be considered at granular levels to paint a more accurate picture. The argument here is also that WFP and the wider community's analysis requires sharpening, with an "early warning" lens in mind at all times, to both prevent and better respond.

WFP and FAO have published two reports based on the IPC to inform the update of the Secretary General to the Security Council on the 2417 Resolution. However, these reports offer an opportunity to bring in deeper analysis. For example, there may be food, but no money to buy food; there is a breakdown of the banking system/non-payment of salaries (*e.g.* Yemen, where the Central Bank was closed, resulting in civil servants and others who received government payments, such as pensioners, not being paid. There is danger in taking refuge in the "shelter of numbers." It can only paint a partial picture.

There are other key shortcomings with the IPC. For one, the IPC is negotiated with, and at times chaired by, the government, which can often be a party to the conflict, thus potentially compromising the principle of neutrality. IPC assumes access—yet, the reality on the ground is that denial-of-humanitarian-access incidents are not overlaid on IPC maps which can distort the picture. IPC is a snapshot that is not a substitute for a qualitative narrative that reflects trends and patterns. It is the latter that is also required, using the 2417 reporting guidance, to support the element of intentionality necessary for prosecution under the Rome Statute. The intention and/or knowledge of wrongdoing, *i.e.* the *mens rea*, is for a litigator to establish. By documenting and reporting to the Security Council, WFP is providing the information necessary for the membership to decide whether it should unilaterally refer a case to the International Criminal Court (ICC). It provides a mechanism to inform member states who can then engage and are obliged to address a situation. The amendment of the Rome Statute was a significant achievement in recognising the destruction of the means for survival as a war crime. Yet it can only be used if a country has ratified the amendment.

WFP can and should support a collective analysis of a situation in line with the Human Rights Up Front initiatives and the Secretary General's Prevention strategy. In addition to the 2417 Resolution, WFP can contribute to the protection of civilians by investing time in the reporting to the Security Council. This can be done through the reports of the Secretary General in integrated mission settings.

Conclusion

The issues at play are complicated and dynamic, and the tools and structures available are not fully utilised. We recommend better analysis, with both qualitative information and quantitative data, of the settings we work in. The relationship between hunger and conflict is complex and dynamic. There are no simple mechanisms or rules. However, one constant lesson from conflicts and countries as diverse as Syria and Sudan is that we need to avoid thinking in terms of a simple binary, a simple cause and effect of hunger following on conflict. Food security is a vital constituent of socio-political security. We ignore this fact to everyone's peril, and the effectiveness of humanitarian response will suffer as a result.

There is a mismatch between the nature and architecture of existing delivery systems and the underlying nature of the need. We recommend that the aid industry rethink its financing, and enable work within a more multilateral framework. To an extent, the tools already exist, *e.g.* multi-partner trust funds.

Existing and evolving juridical frameworks provide means to eliminate the use of hunger as a weapon of war. Accountability mechanisms should be invested in and used, while new accountability frameworks should be seen as opportunities to advocate for support, to better understand the role of food insecurity in the context of the conflict and society concerned, and commit member states to address the use of hunger as a weapon of war.

To end on a positive note, we can do better; many of the challenges outlined above, however diabolical, can only be addressed through a multilateral approach. In the wake of the Rome Statute amendment, there are new accountabilities; just as the means and opportunities exist to take more effective action. This is an urgent task for all concerned by the issue—donors, academics, and practitioners alike.

—Juba, March 2020

Concluding Lecture

H.E. Mr. Simon Coveney, TD

Tánaiste and Minister for Foreign Affairs and Trade

Friends,

We are living through an extraordinarily difficult period in global history.

The arrival of COVID-19 has brought suffering, loss, and hardship to every country, but particularly to those most vulnerable—a stark reminder of our common humanity.

As the World Health Organisation's Dr. Mike Ryan has said, "*no one is safe until everyone is safe,*" a reminder that we are all interdependent. Global safety in the face of the pandemic requires global institutions and a global response. This in turn requires investment in effective multilateralism—the very heart of Irish foreign policy over decades.

At times like these, people need hope. That puts what I call a duty of hope on leaders, though we too need our wellspring from which to take inspiration. The Irish Nobel laureate, Seamus Heaney, once told us:

"If we winter this one out, we can summer anywhere."

Although the calendar tells us it is June and summertime, the virus has plunged the world into winter. But with a collective, coordinated, coherent global response, we will ensure that summer returns.

I do not underestimate the challenge—this is not simply a health crisis but an economic and social one also. It is a test of each of us, our commitment to multilateralism, and of the UN Secretary-General's reform agenda: it is also an opportunity to drive change, to bridge across the humanitarian, development and peace pillars of our work in innovative ways, and to put in place the foundations required for a better future.

We must put in place the foundations for a better future which protects the most vulnerable, those furthest behind.

I am conscious that, while the world is focused on the COVID crisis, we should not forget those already on the margins, living with the stress and strain of conflict, hunger and displacement. The people whom the humanitarian system strives to assist. Those most at risk in a distracted world, a world where resources are scarce and where people are fearful.

That is why Ireland is stepping up.

We are playing our part to help ensure we indeed have that collective, coordinated and coherent global response to COVID-19, with the United Nations at its centre delivering as one.

We are a leading humanitarian donor: the OECD Development Assistance Committee recently observed that Ireland is *"an excellent humanitarian partner"* and that our approaches—informed by Ireland's history of famine and of conflict—could provide a useful inspiration to other donors.

We do as we say—indeed, in that same report, the OECD complimented Ireland for "*walking the talk*" in our focus, making a visible difference and providing leadership, including as a leading advocate for multilateralism.

We draw upon not just our history but also our values, on principles of justice, human rights, the rule of law, and support for peace and friendly cooperation between nations.

That commitment to values, to peace, to the furthest behind—and to doing as we say—is one of the key reasons why Ireland is seeking a seat on the Security Council for 2021-22.

If elected—*when elected*—Ireland will make a difference.

Mary Robinson said at the launch of Ireland's campaign in July 2018, that to seek a seat in the Council is *"the difficult thing."* It would be easier to stand back, to avoid the difficult discussions and hard choices faced by members of the Security Council.

But stepping back and taking the easy option is not the Irish way.

In difficult times, countries like Ireland, which I describe as *"A small country, that thinks big, a country that listens, and a strong independent voice,"* are needed more than ever. On the Security Council, Ireland will be guided by three essential values, those of empathy, independence and partnership, as we play our part in the discharge of the Council's mandate to maintain international peace and security.

As the Secretary-General's recent call for a global ceasefire reminds us, there is a direct connection between peace, security, and reducing humanitarian need. He said, "*There should only be one fight in our world today, our shared battle against COVID-19.*" Yet, even before this crisis, the world faced unprecedented levels of humanitarian need. Today that challenge is even greater—180 million people—and growing, and with it the seeds of potential future conflict and further humanitarian need crises.

The best way to meet humanitarian need is through prevention. Prevention requires us all to step up, to have difficult discussions and to make hard choices. Such discussions are best informed by empathy, independence and partnership. Those Irish values frame this Fordham lecture today, as they have this important series of lectures.

Empathy: Ireland as a Humanitarian Actor

A commitment to helping those in need runs deep in Ireland's culture. Our empathy is born of pain. The pain of discrimination, oppression, and poverty. Of emigration and forced displacement. Of conflict and division. Above all, the huge trauma of our famine, which saw our population reduce by half in only four years.

Our empathy is born from hope—the knowledge that change does come. The Ireland of today is transformed from that of a century ago. I am fortunate to come from a country which is among the best performers on the human development index. I have lived through much of that change.

Ireland's experience has bred in us a fierce desire to help others.

From our experience of conflict and reconciliation grew the desire to help others along the path to peace.

From our experience of injustice and discrimination grew a commitment to shape a multilateral order governed by the rule of law and human rights.

From our experience of hunger grew the impulse to help those furthest behind, first.

These experiences, these impulses helped frame the newly independent Ireland. They inspired a tradition of Irish missionaries, educators and healers. They lay behind the establishment of Irish humanitarian and development NGOs in the 1960s, many of which are now among the most effective worldwide, and Irish Aid, Ireland's official international development programme, now nearly fifty years old.

Irish men and women today express these values daily across the global humanitarian system, here in New York, in Geneva, and in difficult circumstances around the world, working for a better world.

They draw from living tradition.

We remember the Choctaw people. In 1847, from their meagre means, they sent financial assistance to our famine stricken country an ocean away. This was barely sixteen years after the Choctaw faced their own darkest hour on the Trail of Tears.

Their empathy, their solidarity, resonates today.

Seamus Heaney talked of the rhyme of hope and history: they rhymed when an appeal by the Navajo and Hopi nations for support as they coped with the impact of COVID caught the imagination of Irish people who, remembering the historic kindness of the Choctaw, responded to that call spontaneously, in solidarity and with generosity.

That was the spirit which gave birth to Fordham University: founded by an immigrant son of Ireland, John Hughes, to help the poor break the cycle of poverty through education. Hughes bought the original site without having funds to pay for it, relying on the kindness of strangers. Through education, Fordham has helped prepare humanitarians. That is why it has been appropriate that this lecture series has allowed a rich exploration of some of the challenges facing today's humanitarians.

We heard President Higgins and former President Mary Robinson on the challenges of responding to humanitarian needs in the context of human migration and a changing climate.

Practitioners and experts have shared their insights and wisdom.

Dr. Jemilah Mahmood of the International Federation of Red Cross and Red Crescent Societies spoke of the importance of trust in humanitarian action, and the critical role of national and local organisations in building that trust.

Jamie McGoldrick, the Resident and Humanitarian Coordinator for the Occupied Palestinian Territories, shared the challenges of negotiating humanitarian access, particularly in places where non-state actors control territory—and where the act of negotiating such access can potentially criminalise humanitarians.

Dr. Caitriona Dowd of Dublin City University and Matthew Hollingworth of the World Food Programme explored the links between conflict and hunger, and called on us to do more when hunger is used as a weapon of war.

The Chief of Staff of the Irish Defence Forces, Vice Admiral Mark Mellett, discussed the changing nature of peacekeeping and its role in protecting civilians.

A theme across this lecture series has been the need for decision makers to act with empathy. They need to consider how their decisions will resonate across the multilateral system, humanitarian actors, military, governments and other authorities and, above all, those furthest behind, whose voices are the least heard. This is a lesson that Ireland will take with us while serving on the Security Council.

Independence: Ireland as a Champion of Peace, Human Rights, and the Most Vulnerable

The humanitarian principles of independence, neutrality, impartiality and humanity are embedded within Irish foreign policy.

Conflict is the single greatest driver of humanitarian need. In recent years, we have seen conflicts becoming more protracted, more fragmented, and more urbanised. In Syria, Yemen, across the Sahel, and elsewhere, conflicts are dragging on for years, leaving death, misery and the seeds of future mistrust behind.

Such is the scale of misery, of humanitarian need, the world literally cannot afford business as usual.

It is time to muster the global political will to address the root causes of these conflicts. As the Secretary-General said, "*We need robust dip-*

lomatic efforts to meet these challenges." A start would be to implement his appeal for a global ceasefire.

The island of Ireland has known conflict in my lifetime. This has taught us the importance of robust diplomacy to achieving peace. We understand the need for support from friends to enable peace, but also the need to push, to cajole, to encourage and to admonish if peace is to be achieved.

We know too how precious a flame is peace, and the need to nurture and protect it once it has been achieved. Peace can too easily be derailed by continuing misery and need, by the absence of hope.

On the Security Council, Ireland will be a tireless champion of the robust diplomacy of peace.

We bring no selfish interest, no partisan agenda.

We bring neutrality and impartiality.

We bring independence but not indifference.

We bring our informed advocacy.

We bring our experience.

We bring our focus on putting the furthest behind first.

We bring an understanding of the complexities, the geopolitics and the challenges—and the implications of actions, things which cannot simply be wished away. Hard work, informed diplomacy, listening, proposing, and reworking, all in a spirit of collegiality, is required if the minds of the Council are to be focused on moving forward, especially on difficult dossiers.

The work of peace is slow and painstaking. It requires bravery. It come with risk. To be steadfast for peace requires leadership optimistic for the future.

The alternative to working for peace, which I have seen first-hand, is that the jagged splinters of division and violence continue to ruin lives, poison societies, and spread misery.

The Security Council has a duty to create frameworks which facilitate leaders to be steadfast in their pursuit of peace. They can create conditions of hope which allow people to be brave, to take the risks required to build and secure peace.

Of course, delivering on this is not the responsibility solely of Security Council members. Each one of us is called through our global citizenship to help build peace and reduce humanitarian need. That is why Ireland will continue to use our own experiences of conflict and of peacebuilding—our hard won successes, and failures—to support others in their own efforts, just as we were supported during our peace process. This informs Ireland's quiet work, helping to build peace in many places across the world, as well as supporting the efforts of the United Nations including through the Peacebuilding Fund.

Achieving peace also requires stability. That is why Ireland continues to provide strong, practical support to peace keeping and enforcement, holding the proud distinction of being the only nation to have over sixty years continuous deployment on UN, and UN mandated, peace support operations, going back to 1958. Today, Irish peacekeepers are on the ground in Africa, in the Middle East, and in the Balkans.

Ireland also engages constructively across the multilateral system, using our voice and our influence to provide leadership and make a difference. This is particularly important where peace building and humanitarian action meet.

We were proud, with Kenya, to have played an instrumental role in the agreement of the Sustainable Development Goals and Agenda 2030. With Jordan, and drawing on our own experience of emigration, Ireland co-facilitated the New York Declaration on Refugees and Migrants.

Over the last eighteen months, Ireland has chaired the OCHA and ICRC Donor Support Groups, and the CERF advisory board. Ireland complements its engagement with the Peacebuilding Commission with membership of the advisory board of the Peacebuilding Fund. These leadership roles have given us particular insight into the impact of the virus on conflict-affected countries—something which no doubt will impact on the work of the Security Council in the period ahead.

In all of these roles, we have been privileged to work in partnership with others. They will have got to know Ireland's independence, focus and hard work, but particularly the commitment to getting the best result for all.

Partnership—A Belief in the Multilateral System

Effective partnership is the root of Irish foreign policy. Being an island does not make us insular. Quite the opposite—it reminds us of the importance of connections, of working with others to achieve common goals, and of our interdependence with others.

Partnership does not mean homogeneity. It does not mean settling for the lowest common denominator. It requires work. It requires understanding. It requires challenge. It requires a commitment to working towards the highest common factor.

A high functioning multilateral system is the best guarantee of effective partnerships. It is in the multilateral space that the countries of the world come together to work on building those understandings and providing that challenge.

However, any honest reflection on multilateralism today would recognize that we do not always achieve the highest common factor. Each member state has to reflect on why that is.

Effective multilateralism requires wise investments of money, effort and imagination.

It requires patience too—it takes time to deliver change, to build peace, to move up the human development index.

We must also remember that progress is not linear. UNDP say that, as a result of COVID-19, global human development will decline this year for the first time in three decades. The poorest countries, the poorest people, are the most affected.

Addressing this complex knot of crises—health, economic and social—is a test of the multilateral system and of the Secretary-General's reform agenda. It is also a test of the Member States. We must all step up, in partnership. If we do not, unfortunately the risk of destabilisation and conflict increases.

There is good news. The UN global response to COVID-19 has seen the humanitarian and development agencies work effectively together. The new Resident Coordinator system is stepping up.

Ireland has been a strong supporter of that coherent, coordinated UN response—bilaterally, as a committed member of Team Europe and through our leadership within the humanitarian architecture. We have complemented that with Irish support to the Global Fund and GAVI, and our engagement with the International Financial Institutions on such important issues as debt relief. And with this crisis likely to continue, Ireland will stay steadfast in our efforts, our responses and our contributions.

The impact of COVID-19 has been a reminder of the deep interconnection between everybody, every society on Earth. Collective action is helping us tackle the virus and the associated economic and social crises. It is important that we learn lessons from our response, which we can then apply to other challenges such as tackling poverty, inequality or the root causes of extremism.

Those lessons can inform a more effective response to climate change, the great challenge of our age notwithstanding the immediacy of COVID-19. Indeed, climate change is already amplifying the economic and social crises accompanying the virus, at a time when the humanitarian system is stretched to respond to the impacts of conflict, food insecurity and displacement.

Greater consideration needs to be given also to the interplay between climate change and conflict, something with President Robinson has highlighted in this lecture series. She said:

"While no armed conflict has one single driver, there is an increasingly strong body of evidence that suggests that climate change, interacting with other factors, such as political, economic and social conditions, is a major contributing factor."

No country on its own can stop climate change. However, acting together, we can ensure that our children and grandchildren inherit a better world—and we know what we need to do. We have a map. We have a process. We have targets. Working in partnership, we can achieve those targets.

Failure to do so is frightening.

There is, as I said, the risk of increased conflict.

There are island states facing existential threats, which might literally

be under water in our lifetimes.
Food systems will need to change, fast.
There will be increased demand on the humanitarian system.
In addition to our efforts to do better at home, climate action is a cornerstone of Ireland's international development policy. I see delivery on climate action not just as enlightened humanitarianism but, fundamentally, as part of our future national security.
And expanding Ireland's international engagement on climate has deepened our networks, our friendships, including with many other small island states.
We are all aware of the challenges ahead. Addressing climate issues is not easy. It requires difficult trade-offs between today and tomorrow. It requires agile politics. It requires countries to lean in, to trust that others too will make the effort to change, to work in partnership listening to all voices, big and small. This will enable the achievement of optimal solutions to shared problems.
That is why Ireland is a member of the Alliance for Multilateralism, an important investment in the framework enabling and underpinning international trust and partnership. As Helen Keller, a woman who knew so much about triumph through adversity, said, "*Alone we can do so little, together we can do so much.*"

Priorities for the Security Council: IHL, Protection of Civilians, Addressing the Roots of Conflict

Membership of the Security Council brings with it great responsibility. It also provides opportunities to help frame circumstances where humanitarian need can be reduced—or prevented.
Our values of empathy, independence and partnership will inform Ireland's contribution to those elements of the Security Council's work which reduce and prevent humanitarian need, including: ensuring respect for international humanitarian law, and accountability for violations; strengthening the Security Council's work on the protection of civilians; and, addressing the root causes of conflict, and sustaining peace.
For as long as humans have made war, we have made rules to govern

combat, drawing on religion and culture. This was the inspiration for the codification of international humanitarian law in the nineteenth century. These rules are intended to mitigate the effects of conflict on civilians or those who have stopped fighting. They provide the umbrella under which civilians as well as humanitarians can shelter.

Today that shelter is often inadequate—with tragic consequences.

Respect for international humanitarian law is being eroded. When that respect is given, lives are saved. When international humanitarian law is ignored, lives are shattered. Too often we see indiscriminate attacks on civilians, on hospitals, on health workers. We see humanitarians denied lifesaving access. Cruel political games are played with vital permissions repeatedly delayed or refused. And humanitarian aid workers are often deliberately targeted for kidnap or murder.

This is inexcusable.

Peter Maurer, President of the ICRC, spoke at the Security Council on the 70th Anniversary of the Geneva Conventions. He said, "*continued violations of the law do not mean the law is inadequate, but rather that efforts to ensure respect are inadequate.*"

President Maurer urged the Council to do more. I agree.

A key building block in the peace we have achieved on the island of Ireland was building trust in institutions and in the rule of law. Arrangements were put in place to uphold rights and to instil confidence in justice systems.

International humanitarian law needs an investment of analogous confidence building measures. It is essential that members of the Security Council take the lead, calling out breaches of international humanitarian law no matter how uncomfortable the politics. Silence facilitates wrongdoing. By speaking up, by taking action in the face of breaches of international humanitarian law, the Council will save lives not just today but into the future.

We cannot allow a culture of impunity to emerge.

Where international humanitarian law is violated, the Security Council needs to be proactive. It has an important role in ensuring accountability and effective remedy, and in referring certain violations to the International Criminal Court. When countries fail to give effect to the Court's decision, the Council must be seen to act. Arrest warrants must be executed. And this support must be backed up by a renewed commitment to the adequate financing of the Court.

On the Security Council, we will work in partnership to maximise humanitarian space.

There should be no toleration for those who deliberately target humanitarian workers.

While international travel remains complicated by public health restrictions, we need to be vigilant in protecting humanitarian access. We need to watch that it is not deliberately restricted for other motives—indeed, in the face of increasing humanitarian need because of the interlocking health, economic and social crisis, there is a strong argument for prioritising humanitarian access at this time.

We also need to be particularly mindful of the impact of other Security Council decisions on humanitarian space. Our own actions should not undermine humanitarian action.

Sanctions regimes or counter-terrorism measures are essential tools in the Council's armoury. However, when their design does do not take sufficient account of the complexity of humanitarian action during modern conflict it can close the space for principled humanitarian action. And even when that space is kept open, the overhead navigating them imposes on humanitarian organisations—or even the United Nations itself—is too high and itself compromises their ability to respond to need.

Some actors deliberately misinterpret sanctions measures in order to limit or shrink humanitarian space. Humanitarians can be subject to mischievous legal action by elements sympathetic to one or other party to a conflict.

Principled humanitarian action, and brave humanitarians who risk their lives for others, should never be instrumentalised—humanitarians should not have to run the gauntlet of civil or criminal jeopardy.

That is why I believe that in designing sanctions regimes greater consideration must be given to safeguards for humanitarian action.

One way in which we can do this in by keeping our focus firmly on the protection of civilians, a theme which Vice Admiral Mark Mellett explored in his contribution to this lecture series.

Over the last 20 years, the Security Council has worked to develop a 'culture of protection.' Peacekeeping mandates have evolved: the protection of civilians, the intelligent use of sanctions regimes and development of the children and armed conflict agenda have been important, building on the landmark adoption twenty years ago of Resolution 1325, on Women, Peace and Security.

However, there is no room for complacency. As conflict evolves and new conflicts emerge, frequently not involving state actors, fresh protection challenges arise. The Security Council must continue to enhance its work on the protection of civilians, including looking at how its work engages with, and is complementary to, work in other parts of the UN system. For example, can greater complementarity be built between the Council's work on women, peace and security on one hand and that of the Convention on the Elimination of All Forms of Discrimination Against Women (CEDAW) on the other?

We can do more to bridge the gap between the Security Council's stated desire to protect civilians and the translation of that into concrete actions on the ground.

To do this will require difficult discussions. Negotiations for which Ireland is ready, bringing to the table the experience of an island which has only recently emerged from conflict. A conflict in which civilians bore the brunt. And a peace where the role of women negotiators was fundamental to achieving agreement.

We also bring to the Security Council the practical learning from sixty unbroken years of peacekeeping. Our soldiers know the importance of designing peacekeeping mandates which are fit for purpose. Mandates which do not adequately match the realities of conflict on the ground put not just civilians but peacekeepers themselves at risk. Training and resources in turn must match mandates.

Irish peacekeepers have learned how to fully integrate the protection of civilians into policy and practice. Ireland's Defence Forces, through the United Nations Training School Ireland, are at the forefront of ensuring UN peacekeepers are fully trained in the protection of civilians, bringing together troops from across the globe in the Curragh.

These are resources on which we can draw in our contribution to the work of the Security Council.

That practical experience also gives Ireland an insight into the evolving nature of armed conflict, which the Security Council must take into account in its work.

Over the past decade or so, we have seen the terrible humanitarian consequences of urban conflict and, in particular, the effects of explosive weapons in populated areas. New technologies, such as drones or artificial intelligence, mean that human control of weapons is changing. International humanitarian law is trying to keep up. Among the challenges is the toll which explosive weapons have not just on people but also on critical infrastructure.

The destruction of schools means that a generation of children may miss the opportunity for education—and we risk the creation of a new generation of radicals.

The destruction of hospitals means needless deaths, not just from conflict but from otherwise treatable conditions. Conflict related damage to public health systems is affecting the response to COVID-19 in many countries—a danger to their people today but to all of us tomorrow. We have a shared interest in minimising such damage.

The destruction of sanitation systems heightens the incidence of cholera and other diseases.

And the eventual cost of reconstruction is higher, whether the restoration of infrastructure or the rebuilding of lives fractured by conflict.

Every day that systems are under strain is another day when more people somewhere else for safety, whether displaced within their own country or as refugees in another.

It is clear that we cannot be complacent. That is why Ireland is among those leading international efforts in Geneva to address the humanitarian consequences of the use of explosive weapons with wide area effects in populated areas. Consultations began last November on a political declaration which I hope will be concluded in the coming months and which will encourage behavioural change in those who use such explosives. Through enhanced compliance with international humanitarian law adequate to the realities of modern warfare, we will strengthen the protection of civilians.

Of course, the best way to protect civilians from the effects of armed conflict is to avoid conflict in the first place. The Secretary-General's vision on prevention is also Ireland's vision. He said we must "*do everything we can to help countries to avert the outbreak of crises which take a high toll on humanity, undermining institutions and capacities to achieve peace and development.*"

Signs of a looming conflict are apparent in advance. Yet, too often it is only when the first shots are fired, the first wave of people are displaced, or the first massacre occurs that the world starts to take notice. At that stage we find ourselves challenged to respond to humanitarian emergencies, to stabilisation—using funds that would be better invested in development.

That is why I agree with the Secretary-General when he says that "*Prevention must permeate everything we do.*"

This is the philosophy at the heart of Ireland's policy on international development, *A Better World.*

This is the philosophy behind Ireland's contribution to disarmament over many decades.

This is the philosophy which will inform Ireland's contribution to the work of the Security Council.

This understanding is at the heart of Ireland's development policy and the priority we attach to reducing humanitarian need.

While the politics of every conflict are different, many of the warning signs are similar. We need to be attentive to increases in human rights violations and hate speech. Inter-communal violence is a sign that fragility is growing. Conflict in neighbouring states is a danger sign, as is persistent gender inequality and the treatment of women. We are beginning to see climate change impact on security, magnifying the discord which a lack of access to food or wealth can generate. Climate change is creating competition for scarce resources. It is already causing displacement—imagine the displacement should an island have to be evacuated before it disappears.

COVID-19, and the economic consequences of the global shutdown, is placing additional pressures in countries already battling many of these challenges.

I am conscious that there are many places where government structures are very weak. The virus is placing additional pressures on those who wish to stabilise and develop such places. We know also that state absence or weakness is often exploited by armed groups—indeed, we have seen criminal groups in some countries try to use COVID-19 responses to carve out safe areas. In many contexts, armed groups try to become *de facto* authorities, usurping the role of the state as a means to deliver on political objectives. More needs to be done to prevent the hollowing-out of state structures, to prevent the conflicts that inevitably flow from such challenges to state authority.

If we are to deliver on the Charter's ambition to "*save succeeding generations from the scourge of war,*" we must act earlier and with more determination. Preventing conflict, building and sustaining peace must be a priority for the whole UN system. This means that development, humanitarian, human rights and peacebuilding efforts must work together better.

This is the right thing.

This is also the smart thing.

Peacekeeping and humanitarian action costs US$40 billion annually. Imagine what we could achieve if that US$40 billion was invested sustainably and productively?

On the Security Council, Ireland will argue for early, full and effective use of the tools at the Council's disposal, to enable a more comprehensive approach to the prevention of conflict.

This would include deepening the relationship with the Peacebuilding Commission, convening Arria formula meetings, and strategic use of informal meetings so that Security Council debates are seen to be as informed as possible.

We would work to deepen the dialogue and cooperation with regional organisations, to better understand regional dynamics and to improve early warning systems. We are backing this up with a sustained investment in Ireland's bilateral relationships, through my

Government's *Global Ireland* strategy and in Ireland's contribution to effective multilateralism.

Words matter. We would work on the Council to use lines to the press and statements to send the right and timely signals to parties to potential conflict.

I have highlighted the importance of Women, Peace and Security—twenty years on, we have not harnessed the potential of this agenda to prevent conflict. We need more women at the table and in the Security Council chamber. We must work to ensure that women at the table are representative.

On the Security Council, we will listen to women's voices, learn from women's insight, take women's guidance.

We will work to ensure that women must be part of every mandate renewal, of every geographic and thematic discussion, of every local consultation, of every analysis completed in the field. This will make the work of the United Nations even stronger and, importantly, help ensure that where we have achieved peace we help avoid recurrence.

I know from my own involvement in talks in Northern Ireland how difficult, but essential, is the task of sustaining peace. It takes engagement over the long term, patience, ingenuity, imagination and generosity.

Since the adoption of the sustaining peace resolutions in 2016, the Security Council has engaged more deeply in this agenda, whether through discussions on conflict prevention and mediation, or through difficult issues of legacy such as reconciliation, accountability and transitional justice. This is important work, to which Ireland can bring the perspectives and value of lived experience.

Conclusion

Franklin Roosevelt spoke of his hope for "*a better life, a better world, beyond the horizon.*"

It was Roosevelt who first used the phrase 'United Nations.' I like to think that the UN is the vehicle for us to reach that better world, to bring that horizon closer.

The United Nations is us, its member states. We determine how effective it can be. When we step up, the UN steps up. When we act in solidarity, the UN can act in solidarity.

At this moment when the world is facing the triple crisis of COVID -19—health, economic and social—we need our United Nations to be at its most effective. That will enable the best possible response to the humanitarian consequences of this crisis. To get there, each of must contribute to a renewed global solidarity.

Ireland will play our part in building that solidarity, bringing our values of empathy, partnership and independence, our history and our hard work. We will do so in the plenary halls of New York and Geneva, on the boards and in the backrooms, in capitals and, we hope, on the Security Council.

With a clear, strong and independent voice, we will keep people at the centre of all our efforts and seek to leave no one behind.

—Dublin, May 2020

About

The Permanent Mission of Ireland to the UN

The role of the Permanent Mission of Ireland to the UN is to promote Ireland's foreign policy interests and values at the UN and, through the UN, to promote effective international action on a range of global issues. The team, led by Ireland's Permanent Representative, Ambassador Geraldine Byrne Nason, works to represent Ireland and to ensure that Ireland's voice is heard in the global forum in order to make a difference where it matters. Ireland has kept faith with the UN since joining in 1955 as a young Republic and continues to consider membership of the UN as a fundamental pillar of Irish foreign policy and to global peace and security.

The Institute of International Humanitarian Affairs

The Institute of International Humanitarian Affairs (IIHA) prepares current and future aid workers with the knowledge and skills needed to respond effectively in times of humanitarian crisis and disaster. Our courses are borne of an interdisciplinary curriculum that combines academic theory with the practical experience of seasoned humanitarian professionals. The IIHA also publishes on a wide range of humanitarian topics and regularly hosts a number of events in the New York area, including the annual Humanitarian Blockchain Summit and Design for Humanity Summit.

The Refuge Press

The Refuge Press is the publishing arm of Fordham University's Institute of International Humanitarian Affairs. It is our independent imprint in partnership with Fordham University Press. The Refuge Press publishes primarily in three areas: Changing Perceptions, Lifting Voices from Forgotten Crises, Reflections on Our Time.

Fordham University

Founded in 1841, Fordham is the Jesuit University of New York, offering exceptional education distinguished by the Jesuit tradition across nine schools. Fordham awards baccalaureate, graduate, and professional degrees to approximately 15,000 students from Fordham College at Rose Hill, Fordham College at Lincoln Center, the Gabelli School of Business (undergraduate and graduate), the School of Professional and Continuing Studies, the Graduate Schools of Arts and Sciences, Education, Religion and Religious Education, and Social Service, and the School of Law. The University has residential campuses in the Bronx and Manhattan, a campus in West Harrison, N.Y., the Louis Calder Center Biological Field Station in Armonk, N.Y., and the London Centre in the United Kingdom.

Contributing Authors

Geraldine Byrne Nason
Permanent Representative of Ireland to the United Nations
Prior to her appointment to the United Nations in 2017, Ambassador Nason served as Ireland's Ambassador to France and Monaco and as Second Secretary-General in the Department of Taoiseach. A career diplomat, she served as Deputy Permanent Representative to the European Union, headed Ireland's Nations Forum on Europe, and was Director for Governance at the Organisation for Economic Cooperation and Development (OECD) in Paris.

Brendan Cahill
Executive Director, Institute of International Humanitarian Affairs, Fordham University
For nearly twenty years Mr. Cahill has created, directed and taught humanitarian programs worldwide. He established and leads Fordham University's undergraduate and graduate programs in Humanitarian Studies. He founded The Refuge Press, of which he serves as Publisher.

Mary Robinson
Chair of The Elders
H.E. Mary Robinson was the first woman elected President of Ireland. She stepped down from this position to serve as U.N. High Commissioner for Human Rights. She is the Founder and current President of the Mary Robinson Foundation for Climate Justice.

Michael D. Higgins
President of Ireland
President Michael D. Higgins is currently serving his second term as the ninth president of Ireland. He previously held positions as Ireland's first Minister for Arts, Culture and the Gaeltacht. President Higgins is a poet and writer, academic and statesman, human rights advocate, and champion of creativity within Irish society.

Jemilah Mahmood, MD
Under Secretary General for Partnerships, International Federation of Red Cross and Red Crescent Societies
Prior to joining IFRC in 2016, Dr. Mahmood served as the Chief of the World Humanitarian Summit secretariat at the United Nations. She is well known as the founder of MERCY Malaysia; her previous appointments include being Chief of the Humanitarian Response Branch at UNFPA, Senior Fellow at Khazanah Nasional in Malaysia's Khazanah Research and Investment Strategy Division, and Senior Visiting Research Fellow at the Humanitarian Futures Programme at Kings College in London.

Vice Admiral Mark Mellett DSM, PhD
Chief of Staff of the Irish Defence Forces
With over forty years of service in the Irish Defence Forces, he is the first naval officer in the Irish State to serve as Chief of Staff, having previously served as Deputy Chief of Staff and Chief of Navy. He began his military career as an army reservist, before being selected for a naval cadetship in the Permanent Defence Forces. He was the second Naval Officer in the history of the Irish State to be awarded *"The Distinguished Service Medal (DSM)"* by the Irish Government for his leadership of a complex maritime narcotics interdiction operation.

Jamie McGoldrick
United Nations Deputy Special Coordinator for the Middle East Peace Process, Resident Coordinator and Humanitarian Coordinator for the Occupied Palestinian Territory
Prior to his appointment in 2015, Mr. McGoldrick served as the United Nations Resident Coordinator, Humanitarian Coordinator and United Nations Development Programme (UNDP) Resident Representative in Yemen. He assumed that position after serving as the Resident and Humanitarian Coordinator, and the UNDP Resident Representative in Nepal (2013-2015) and Resident Coordinator and Resident Representative of UNDP in Georgia (2009-2013).

Caitriona Dowd, PhD

Assistant Professor in Security Studies, Dublin City University

Dr. Dowd's research concerns the dynamics of political violence in sub-Saharan Africa, with particular attention to the targeting of civilians in humanitarian crises, and the use of new and emerging methodologies for violence monitoring. Previously a peace and conflict specialist in the humanitarian sector, Dr. Dowd has worked in Afghanistan, Central African Republic, Ethiopia, Kenya, Mali, Nigeria, Somalia and South Sudan, among others.

Matthew Hollingworth

United Nations World Food Program Country Director and Representative in South Sudan

Mr. Hollingworth has worked for the WFP for 19 years. Prior to taking up his current position, he served as the Country Director and Representative in Sudan, the Deputy Regional Director for the Middle East, North Africa, Central Asia and Eastern Europe, and the Country Director and Representative for WFP operations in war-torn Syria.

Anne-Laure Duval

Global Head of Protection at the World Food Programme

Prior to taking up her current position in 2019, Ms. Duval worked for the WFP as the Deputy Head of the Regional facility in Amman and Chief of Staff of the Sudan Country Office. Ms. Duval's previous international positions include working for the Council of Europe, the United Nations Department of Peacekeeping Operations; the New Zealand Aid Programme, and World Vision.

Simon Coveney, TD

Tánaiste of Ireland and Minister of Foreign Affairs and Trade

Tánaiste Simon Coveney currently serves as Deputy Leader of Fine Gael. Prior to taking up his current appointments in 2017, he served as Minister for Housing, Planning and Local Government; Minister for Agriculture, Food and the Marine; and Chaired the EU Council of Agriculture and Fisheries Ministers.

Endnotes

1. UN (2018) '"No other conclusion," ethnic cleansing of Rohingyas in Myanmar continues - senior UN rights official,' 6 March 2018, https://news.un.org/en/story/2018/03/1004232 *

2. UN (2019) 'Collective drive to end hunger, malnutrition "in reverse" since 2015, Deputy Secretary-General says at event on transforming food systems' 25 September 2019, available at https://www.un.org/press/en/2019/dsgsm1342.doc.htm *

3. FSIN (2019) Global Report on Food Crises.

4. FAO (2017) The Future of Food and Agriculture: Trends and Challenges.

5. FAO (2016) Peace and Food Security: Investing in Resilience to Sustain Rural Livelihoods amid Conflict.

6. See Starvation Accountability, 'Mass Starvation Expert Report' available at https://starvationaccountability.org/resources/expert-report *

7. Concern Worldwide (2018) Conflict and Hunger: The Lived Experience of Conflict and Food Insecurity in South Sudan, https://www.concern.net/insights/conflict-and-hunger-lived-experience-conflict-and-food-insecurity-south-sudan.

8. President Michael D. Higgins (2019), Ireland at Fordham Humanitarian Lecture Series, available at https://medium.com/humanitarianpulse/president-of-ireland-michael-d-c88a98e1a72b *

9. Hunger Task Force (2008) Hunger Task Force Report, https://www.irishaid.ie/news-publications/publications/publicationsarchive/2008/september/hunger-task-force-report/, p.6.

10. Department of Foreign Affairs and Trade (2019) Ireland's Third National Action Plan on Women, Peace and Security https://www.dfa.ie/media/dfa/ourrolepolicies/womenpeaceandsecurity/Third-National-Action-Plan.pdf

11. Caitlin Hamilton, Nyibeny Naam and Laura J. Shepherd (2020). Twenty Years of Women, Peace and Security National Action Plans: Analysis and Lessons Learned, database at www.wpsnaps.org *

12. Bell, Christine, Sanja Badanjak, Juline Beujouan, Robert Forster, Tim Epple, Astrid Jamar, Kevin McNicholl, Sean Molloy, Kathryn Nash, Jan Pospisil, Robert Wilson, Laura Wise (2020). PA-X Codebook, Version 3. Political Settlements Research Programme, University of Edinburgh, Edinburgh. Available at https://www.peaceagreements.org/ *

13. UN Security Council Resolution 2417 Protection of Civilians in Armed Conflict (2018) http://unscr.com/en/resolutions/2417 **

14. Last https://www.icc-cpi.int/NR/rdonlyres/EA9AEFF7-5752-4F84-BE94-0A655EB30E16/0/Rome_Statute_English.pdf ** See also http://opiniojuris.org/2019/12/07/the-rome-statutes-flawed-amendment-regime-starvation-in-niac-edition/ **

15. See International Committee for the Red Cross (ICRC), Rule 53. The use of starvation of the civilian population as a method of warfare is prohibited, Customary International Law Database (applying to both international and non-international law contexts).

16. https://www.newstatesman.com/books/2011/01/world-war-food-hunger-million Lizzie Collingham, (2011) in The Taste of War: World War II and the Battle for Food (Introduction – War and Food) [Last accessed 15 January 2020]

17. https://sites.tufts.edu/wpf/famine/ **

18. WFP was established in 1961 after the 1960 Food and Agriculture Organization (FAO) Conference, when George McGovern, director of the US Food for Peace Programmes, proposed establishing a multilateral food aid programme. The WFP was formally established in 1963 by the FAO and the United Nations General Assembly on a three-year experimental basis. In 1965, the programme was extended to a continuing basis.

19. https://www.wfp.org/history **

20. Josette Sheeran, Executive Director, United Nations' World Food Programme, the Economist, November, 2007.

21. World Food Summit 1996, Food security is "a situation that exists when all people, at all times, have physical, social and economic access to sufficient, safe and nutritious food that meets their dietary needs and food references for an active and healthy life." http://www.fao.org/3/y4671e/y4671e06.htm **

22. United Nations Human Rights Committee, General Comment 12 on the Right to Food (1999) https://www.refworld.org/docid/4538838c11.html **

23. https://www.wfp.org/publications/wfp-humanitarian-protection-policy **

24. https://interagencystandingcommittee.org/protection-priority-global-protection-cluster/documents/iasc-policy-protection-humanitarian-action **

25. Paul F. Diehl, Just a Phase?: Integrating Conflict Dynamics Over Time, Conflict Management and Peace Science, 23:3, 199-210,(2006) https://journals.sagepub.com/doi/10.1080/07388940600837490 **

26. Food Security & Sociopolitical Stability, at 4, (2016) (Christopher B. Barrett, ed.)

27. Phonetically: Aish horriah Aadaleh Igtimaeiah; https://www.youtube.com/watch?v=Y9Re4zJkoQM

28. https://www.middleeasteye.net/news/out-movie-idlibs-farmers-find-themselves-victims-scorched-earth-campaign **

29. Indicated throughout the report of Independent International Commission of Inquiry on the Syrian Arab Republic https://www.ohchr.org/Documents/HRBodies/HRCouncil/CoISyria/A-HRC-37-72_EN.pdf

30. See Alex de Waal and Bridget Conley, The Purposes of Starvation: Historical and Contemporary Uses at 710 in the Journal of International Criminal Justice 17 (2019), 699-722. Also noting that "mass starvation is a process of deprivation that occurs when actors impede the capacity of targeted persons to access the means of sustaining life.", at 699.

31. https://www.unhcr.org/news/latest/2015/7/559bdb0e6/225-million-displaced-south-sudan-across-its-borders.html **

32. https://odihpn.org/magazine/protection-civilians-poc-sites-impact-broader/ **

33. Para. 27 https://reliefweb.int/sites/reliefweb.int/files/resources/Accountability%20for%20Starvation-South%20Sudan.pdf **

34. Ibid.

35. Alex de Waal, The Real Politics of the Horn of Africa, at 54 (2015).

36. Ibid.

37. https://www.state.gov/state-sponsors-of-terrorism/ **

38. https://reliefweb.int/report/world/humanitarian-development-peace-nexus-what-does-it-mean-multi-mandated-organizations **

39. See: https://www.agendaforhumanity.org/initiatives/3861 **

40. https://www.oecd.org/dac/effectiveness/34428351.pdf **

41. https://www.oecd.org/dac/effectiveness/49650173.pdf **

42. https://www.oecd.org/dac/conflict-fragility-resilience/incaf-network.htm **

43. See e.g. WFP's contribution on peace and conflict prevention through its in diverse situations, including outright violent conflict and transition from violence to sustainable peace, INCAF, DAC Meeting, 18 November 2019 http://www.oecd.org/officialdocuments/publicdisplaydocumentpdf/?cote=DCD/DAC/RD(2019)9&docLanguage=En **

44. https://www.un.org/un70/en/content/videos/three-pillars/index.html **

45. UN Security Council Resolution 2417 (2018), supra note 1.

46. Famine early warning and information systems in conflict settings: challenges for humanitarian metrics and response.http://eprints.lse.ac.uk/102836/Daniel Maxwell, (2019) Famine early warning and information systems in conflict settings: challenges for humanitarian metrics and response. Conflict Research Programme, London School of Economics and Political Science, London, UK.

47. Determining famine: Multi-dimensional analysis for the twenty-first century (Daniel Maxwell, Abdullahi Khalif, Peter Hailey and Francesco Checchi), 2020.

48. http://www.fao.org/3/ca3113en/CA3113EN.pdf **

49. https://sites.tufts.edu/reinventingpeace/files/2019/09/Accountability-for-Starvation-Crimes-Yemen.pdf, at 5 **

50. http://www.irishtimes.com/culture/books/hunger-the-ugly-truth-about-the-world-s-oldest-problem-1.4178375?mode=amp. **

51. https://interagencystandingcommittee.org/system/files/overview_of_human_rights_up_front_july_2015.pdf **

52. https://www.un.org/sg/en/priorities/prevention.shtml **

53. https://documents.wfp.org/stellent/groups/public/documents/govman/wfp268162.pdf **

* [Last accessed 25 March 2020]
** [Last accessed on 2 April 2020]